PRAISE FOR *ARIZONA FRIEND TRIPS*

"Lisa Schnebly Heidinger and Julie Morrison have a saying: the making of a true Arizona woman is measured not in her femininity but in her fierceness. And their love for this state is fierce indeed. Come along on this journey with them to see multiple corners of Arizona in a whole new way."

—**TOM ZOELLNER**, AUTHOR OF *RIM TO RIVER: LOOKING INTO THE HEART OF ARIZONA*

"If ever there was a love letter written to the state of Arizona, this is it. . . . *Arizona Friend Trips* is a celebration of friendship, history, and the beauty of Arizona, which can only be appreciated by those who are willing to stop, slow down, and gaze."

—**OLIVIA FIERRO**, OLIVIA'S BOOK CLUB, PHOENIX

"Lisa Schnebly Heidinger recapitulates her ancestral Arizona roots through her travels with poet Julie Morrison, also a native. Their impressionistic pilgrimages evoke a deepening friendship tinged with nostalgia. Heidinger's photos and essays, complemented by Morrison's commemorative poetry, present a powerful geography of Arizona in a deeply personal, emotional tribute to their native state."

—**DAVID YETMAN**, HOST AND PRODUCER OF *IN THE AMERICAS WITH DAVID YETMAN* ON PBS

"An unforgettable paean to places held deep in the hearts of these two magnificent Arizona women. Drink in the poetry, the prose, the photographs, the eloquent and courageous sharing of souls. You will fall in love with their places, and you won't be able to help falling just a little in love with them as well."

—**DAVID MCCUMBER**, EXECUTIVE EDITOR, *ARIZONA DAILY STAR*

"*Arizona Friend Trips* is a nontraditional guidebook that entices readers to explore Arizona. In a series of personal essays, photos, poems, and quips, the authors take us on a road trip to experience some of Arizona's quirkiest and most iconic sights. This is not a traditional guidebook—you won't learn how to get from Point A to Point B in its pages—but you will learn something about why you should go. And you might even decide to take a friend along for the ride."

—**JULIE HAMMONDS**, SOULSTICE PUBLISHING

"Follow friends Heidinger and Morrison on an epic yet personal journey along the blue highways and faraway trails of their beloved home state of Arizona. With prose, poetry, and photography, we are taken on an insider's expedition through the great places of legend, myth, and history, and experience Arizona's iconic landscapes and diverse cultures through the eyes and hearts of two daughters of the desert."

—**LESLEY POLING-KEMPES**, AUTHOR OF *LADIES OF THE CANYONS: A LEAGUE OF EXTRAORDINARY WOMEN AND THEIR ADVENTURES IN THE AMERICAN SOUTHWEST*

ARIZONA FRIEND TRIPS

PROSE AND PHOTOS BY
LISA SCHNEBLY HEIDINGER

POETRY BY
JULIE MORRISON

Arizona Friend Trips

STORIES FROM THE ROAD

THE UNIVERSITY OF
ARIZONA PRESS
TUCSON

The University of Arizona Press
www.uapress.arizona.edu

We respectfully acknowledge the University of Arizona is on the land and territories of Indigenous peoples. Today, Arizona is home to twenty-two federally recognized tribes, with Tucson being home to the O'odham and the Yaqui. Committed to diversity and inclusion, the University strives to build sustainable relationships with sovereign Native Nations and Indigenous communities through education offerings, partnerships, and community service.

ISBN-13: 978-0-8165-5370-9 (paperback)
ISBN-13: 978-0-8165-5371-6 (ebook)

Cover design by Emily Weigel
Cover photograph by Lisa Schnebly Heidinger
Designed and typeset by Leigh McDonald in Bell MT 10.5/14 and Eldon WF (display)

Library of Congress Cataloging-in-Publication Data
Names: Heidinger, Lisa Schnebly, author. | Morrison, Julie, author.
Title: Arizona friend trips : stories from the road / prose and photos by Lisa Schnebly Heidinger ; poetry by Julie Morrison.
Description: Tucson : University of Arizona Press, 2025.
Identifiers: LCCN 2024025403 (print) | LCCN 2024025404 (ebook) | ISBN 9780816553709 (paperback) | ISBN 9780816553716 (ebook)
Subjects: LCSH: Automobile travel—Arizona—Guidebooks. | Arizona—Description and travel—Guidebooks. | LCGFT: Guidebooks.
Classification: LCC F809.3 .H45 2025 (print) | LCC F809.3 (ebook) | DDC 917.9104—dc23/eng/20241031
LC record available at https://lccn.loc.gov/2024025403
LC ebook record available at https://lccn.loc.gov/2024025404

Printed in the United States of America
♾ This paper meets the requirements of ANSI/NISO Z39.48-1992 (Permanence of Paper).

For Larry Schnebly,
whose words stay with us

Larry Schnebly by the Colorado River.

CONTENTS BY THE COMPASS

HEADING SOUTHEAST

HEADING SOUTH

HEADING SOUTHWEST

HEADING WEST

CENTRAL

HEADING NORTHWEST

HEADING NORTH CENTRAL

Our Monument Valley trip.

READY, SET, ROAD TRIP!

Story Maps

We were born and grown here,
from families long established—
people of a past that's all but vanished—
retold tellings echo in our ears.

From forebears' lives and land we came,
though we've written our own stories,
lifelines melding territory,
identity a state as well as name.

We learned while navigating—
journeys, visits, points of interest—
spaces change us with a visit—
living memory creating.

Whether for the first time or to repeat trips past,
we road-tripped to places still shaping our maps.

And a prose note from the poet:

Both text and photos follow a compass rather than chronology. Dogs, for example, lived and traveled as Ranger and Lucy in our earliest trips, then just Lucy, then Lucy and Augie, and, finally, just Augie, but when grouped by direction of trips, they come and go out of order in a way that may be confusing. Not to worry: the dogs knew where they were at all times, even if the same cannot be said of us.

HOW WE GOT HERE

Few people I know resonate as strongly with the "go in the car" impulse as I do (I call it the red-setter gene), so finding out that Julie Morrison was one of us was an early pleasure in our friendship. It was Julie who suggested that since we both have that deep love of road trips, are both descendants of Arizona pioneer families, both fiercely cherish our state even on its worst days, and both love writing, we could collaborate on a book.

We decided to visit places we've seen separately that have resonated with one of us, as well as places we've mentioned in mutually reverent tones. Julie would write poems, and I would contribute text and photos.

Well, we did. You're seeing the result of those excursions.

You can learn a lot about people by traveling with them in any manner, and I think perhaps most during hours on asphalt. We were delighted to discover that even under grueling circumstances, our interactions never suffered. We mutually gloried in the two-lanes my dad Larry called "blue highways," appreciated swift passage on newer widened roads (and my gosh, all the passing lanes on 89 North are a gift to motorists), and savored sights both remembered and revised since we'd last seen them. Julie got to meet Larry, my father, at the storied Arizona Inn, and they each swiftly grasped why the other meant so much to me. I quoted him so often to her that she made many of his words part of her vernacular. Since his passing at ninety-four, she has kept his spirit alive with me.

Larry and Julie are the only two people with whom travel was effortless for me. Julie and I, like Larry and I, got so tired that things seemed even funnier. With her, "this should go on the t-shirt" became the signal that a particular line merited keeping. We've included some of those lines in each section. I learned Julie is a true Arizona woman, which means her femininity is measured not in frailty but in fierceness: she is tirelessly dedicated to her passions (which include her dogs, her people, and her writing), and plunges herself fully into each experience. She also has a grand laugh.

As an author, I sometimes struggle with wondering what hubris leads me to believe the world needs any words I might have; doesn't each traveler have a similar set of thoughts, impressions, and opinions? Upon reflection, I decided that indeed, any traveler might, and I would love to read anything they wrote about such journeys. So, if you write such a book, please let me know.

In the meantime, you're getting a patchwork of places, some beloved to both Julie and me, and some new to one or the other of us. You're getting feelings, thoughts, recalled anecdotes—pretty much anything except recipes. (That's someone else's book.) And I hope you enjoy accompanying us on the road trips that resulted in these written and photographic memories even a tenth as much as we savored the days of discovery, then debriefing about them afterward. It's not nothin', as we've come to say, to not only want to talk after long days in the car but continue to appreciate and even marvel at the results of such times. I count myself among the most fortunate of people to have made this volume with Julie.

ARIZONA FRIEND TRIPS

View from the Grand Canyon's North Rim.

HEADING NORTH

NORTH RIM

With Augie on the trail.

Perspective

Eventually you learn that you don't draw a circle,
you draw the light around a circle.
—ANNIE MCELRATH, ARTIST AND POET

Present a place with too much shine
and experience slips, esteem falls,
smattering disappointment.

The Grand Canyon, for me,
had never been great as its name
until seen from a different side,
colors grading, refracting into lines
smudging, shading, sketching,
North Rim an artist playing with blues
while its southern sibling flashes red.

Cool, here, is plain air ease, winking,
haze and echo waltzing into sky
untroubled by time,
space to lapse, laze, wonder
at purple walls, color rising, falling—
a pulse in relief—
these depths draw
setting me at such a height
that descent doesn't mean coming down.
My perspective is too different now:
down is up, this isn't beauty,
this is what beauty is trying to be,
so there can be no coming down,
only a return.

"Every trait has a good side and a bad side."
—Lisa, at our zeal for seeing something because "we've come this far" or "it's just not that out of the way."

NORTH RIM

The first three times I went to the North Rim, I was working.

Half a lifetime ago I drove up with Channel 3 photographer Mike Schmidt to shoot a piece. After getting an interview with an employee and making sure Mike got video of what I wanted to describe, we looked at the canyon. But I didn't gaze at the canyon; there wasn't time (which reminds me of a venerable newsman wryly remarking about breaking news hysteria, "Thinking? There isn't time!")

Then my dad, Larry, went with me to do a story for *Arizona Highways* about Colorado City, looking after my one-year-old daughter, Sedona, while I did interviews. We came to the North Rim on the way back. Running along the trail with Sedona in the rattly little portable stroller was a good metaphor for that trip. I could see the scenery, but I mostly saw her—in this case, making sure she didn't careen off the edge because I wasn't paying attention. A vacation with a small child is a business trip: you're not home, but you're working. She loved the bronze statue of Brighty, even though lacking the language to discuss who he was.

The third time, Larry and Sedona and I returned, and my son, Rye, was also along, six when Sedona was eight. They bravely walked the trail to Ed Abbey's fire tower so I could write about that. This time they both greeted Brighty, noticing his nose was gold from rubbed greetings while the rest of him was dark bronze. We'd read the book about him aloud in the week leading up to the trip. We stayed in a cabin with a fireplace and front porch, and Sedona and Rye had a pillow fight with my dad, which may have been their best-remembered part of the trip.

This fourth trip was for work in a way, except that this book is more play. And, with Julie, I did take time to gaze; this time she was the one on a bit of a business trip, with Augie along. But Augie's less time-intensive than a human child, so we both got gazing time.

We stopped to check in at the Jacob Lake Lodge (we would discover the next morning that the only indication of where Jacob Lake itself had

View from a room by the North Rim Trail.

been was a wooden sign in a slightly lower section of meadow.) Once we got past the charred desolation of the Kaibab after a fire, which made us sad, we absorbed the forest, so different from the one you drive through approaching the South Rim. There it's piñon and juniper with ponderosa pine. Here ponderosa shares space with Douglas fir and blue spruce.

Only 10 percent of the people who visit the Grand Canyon see it from the north. You need time off for a long drive; you need a vehicle you can trust. Those who do come find parking places more easily, don't push through as much of a crowd to get a seat on the veranda, and don't meet as many people on the trail.

All those contributed to why Julie vastly preferred the North Rim. Walking with her and Augie, I got to register what a different view you get looking south.

From the South Rim, the canyon's pretty much all laid out in front of you, as far as you can see. From the North Rim, views only go to the next curve. It's tucked in, intimate. From the South Rim, everything is shades of rust and rose, seeping into deeper tones at sunset. From the North Rim, blues and greens prevail. The South Rim brims with commerce, and I love layers of saved recollections laid down over decades, even in the commercial buildings: Kolb Studio, Desert View Watchtower, El Tovar, and Bright

Angel. But here, the lodge is it. Meals in the dining room are amazing but didn't fit in our schedule on this trip. It's always good to have something to look forward to doing the next time. No choices, no shopping, no distractions. We gazed at the canyon.

I'd hoped to re-create a photo from years ago that showed the far-off silhouette of the San Francisco Peaks through the soaring lodge windows, but summer's haze hid them. Instead, we found a new delightful photo, from a rock room constructed just for looking out of. Purity of purpose made it even more charming. We could have stayed there for hours, but Jacob's Lake Inn was waiting for us.

All in all in all, as my husband says, the North Rim is quieter, more meandering. It's subtle compared to the South Rim experience, which can almost yell, "Check this out!" The North Rim murmurs the invitation.

"You can't leave a place you haven't been."
—Lisa, quoting Steve Chandler explaining the process of discerning feelings.

Paria River, near Lonely Dell.

LEES FERRY

What Hope Is There?

How would hope appear here?
Where light scalds and water is moody—
meetings more crossing than confluence—
at the base of cliffs, does hope rise
high enough to clear walls?
Get stuck as a steering oar
between unknown hazards?
Was hope the bonnet donned,
sure to wear, fade, fray,
perhaps beyond mending?
A plank bolted against attack?
At least, a surprise bloom,
at most the daily grit
silting food, wash, views
best learned to live with?

"Best view, worst house."
—Lisa's summation of Emma Lee's homestead.

LEES FERRY

Of all Arizona's wonderful places, this may be my most treasured.

Lees Ferry brings you through a wild collection of jumbled scenery on the road to the perfect reward: you can walk into the Colorado River. Which, unless you pay for a boat trip, you really can't do many other places. There are docks at Lakes Mead and Powell, but that's not the same, and by Yuma it's a greatly reduced version of the rollicking, uproarious waves just below the put-in here.

On the way you've passed the imposing Echo Cliffs, over which the Honeymoon Trail from eastern Arizona crept back up to Saint George in Utah, where Mormon couples could be joined for eternity. You've driven through the striated hummocks—which we've long called the Land of the Mole People—after leaving Cameron, and finally passed the hoodoos, rocks shaped into Dr. Suess–like sculptures by wind. Finally, the Colorado River. Having put in from here for three raft trips imbues this place with reverence to me. Once you take that trip, you are never the same, and this is the baptismal site.

That said, the Colorado River is only a slice of the whole Lees Ferry pie that beguiles me so. Lonely Dell Ranch, where John D. Lee's wife Emma lived a remarkable life, provides a lot of the wonder.

The first time I made the short hike from the River (capitalized out of reverence) to the old homestead (now a National Park Service site), it was so our first river guide could put some distance between us and another boat departing at the time. We walked under broiling sun up the dusty track to see the little farm nestled at the foot of Vermilion Cliffs. (A very privileged but someone sheltered young woman asked him sincerely, "Are those colors natural?" Our guide managed to answer with a straight face that they were.)

Emma Lee was one of John D.'s nineteen wives, and the most steadfast: when he was tried for his part in the Mountain Meadows Massacre, she was the one who visited him in jail, wrote letters for him, brought him food. I remember my dad marveling at her devotion since he took a dim

Emma Lee's root cellar.

view of John D.'s constant travel. Emma gave birth alone, twice, here in the one-room shelter. What kind of husband lets that happen?

But that's also why I admire Emma so: as labor intensified, she sent the other children out to play, probably trying not to cry out and frighten them. She was the catalyst for my belief that in Arizona, femininity is measured not in fragility but in strength. She also took her children down to a riverbank camp when a Navajo chief brought his party through. After feeding them dinner, she claimed she felt uneasy, and boldly approached the chief to ask for protection through the night. Impressed, he put the word out to his people across the area to leave her alone.

Julie and I are here to pay homage to womanly courage, looking at the stacked sandstone root cellar and the two buildings Emma used. To my dismay, they have been "improved" into a sterile and more modern version of their authentic selves, with new roofs. Likewise have the small tombstones with the names of the Johnson children, buried within a few days of one another, been replaced with new versions (the Johnsons having replaced Emma at the ferry after John D. was shot into his coffin at Mountain Meadows). A family heading back east after losing children to diphtheria had given the Lees their old clothing and blankets. Four of the family's children perished from that well-intentioned germ-sharing.

While I mourn the authenticity of the old markers, these new modern ones remind me that our impressions are shaped by at what stop we board the historical bus. For me, these changes are indulgences by the living that desecrate the efforts of the dead. But someone visiting for the first time can still peer into the cool depths of Emma's root cellar and probably feel more connected than disappointed.

Perhaps to offset my regret, Julie suggests we follow the Paria River back from the homesite. This is all new territory for us both. With the dogs, we take in the old corral, the picturesque pickup, and gorgeous bends in the river, shimmering in shades of opal as it is lit by setting sun.

The Paria's high alkalinity is probably what killed Emma's fruit trees; now they flourish under rangers' care and presumably a different irrigation source. The orchards are another newer addition to an old site, but since they didn't tear out old trees and put in new ones, I don't mind that.

What matters most to me about Lonely Dell is that it's where Emma persevered. She continued to carry water to the last little peach tree in her orchard until it died because it simply wasn't in her to give up. The image of that determined strength is what I take away with me every time I visit.

"Blessings come to us, or come through us."
—Julie, quoting a(nother) dear friend when reasons for odd
or inexplicable events remain a mystery.

NAVAJO BRIDGE

.arry Schnebly remembering dropping echo rocks with his father.

Banks and Bridges

As a junior transportation planner,
I was dispatched to Alaska
assessing transit options
to a "bridge to nowhere."

The opposite bank
from the city's anchorage
was unpopulated forest,
to a naturalist, sleepy and green,
to a developer, ripe for new growth.

As massive investments,
bridges must justify themselves
through equal or greater values
of increases in trade, employment, or
advancement of human capital.

The options were a ferry or a bus:
mostly human—instead of money—movers
with differing costs.

Both were unpopular, and me, more so,
because of economic hopes
not only banked, but attracting interest:
money has its own gravity,
and this region had felt like a satellite
for too long.

An arduous process decided
the best alternative
was none at all:
ironically,
the pro-bridge lead agency
could neither circumnavigate,
nor make a lasting connection,
that people would ever live or work
on an empty bank.

Thus, I learned a question—
for both sides at a distance—
what's banked that merits bridging?

"When I was here with Larry . . ."
—Lisa. Almost every trip.

NAVAJO BRIDGE

As if there weren't enough to love about the Navajo Bridge, it is the same age as my father. That always made it special to him, which makes it special to me.

Julie and I are here to look for condors; the last time she came, there were several sitting in the massive metal joints under the bridge. Since the new bridge opened next door to this one in 1995, visitors have been able to walk out on the old one. (They're both called the Navajo Bridge now, with "historic" added to the original one's title to differentiate.)

I first became aware of this one at another historic bridge—the charming old span that crosses the Little Colorado at Cameron. That one, built in 1911, was quaintly damaged in 1937 when too many sheep crossed at once. Replaced in 1959 by the one we drive over on U.S. 89, looking at the Cameron bridge reminded my father of the Navajo Bridge we would cross later the same day, and he told me this story.

On Larry's way to be dropped off at Wasatch Academy in Mount Pleasant, Utah, his father stopped at the Cameron bridge and instructed him to pick up a half-dozen or so big flat sandstone rocks. He wouldn't tell him why. Then, at Navajo Bridge, they crossed over, parked, and walked back out on what was then a very scarcely traveled metal crossing. His dad told him to drop the first rock.

Against the background of red sandstone cliffs, the rock disappeared from sight. But then, they heard the splash, and the echoes: crack-shot, two, three, four. My dad ran for the next rock. Big ones sometimes yielded more echoes. He was a Navajo Bridge fan from that day on.

Julie and I look down at the river. As always, I'm entranced by being so close to the Colorado. From this point, amazing adventures await river runners. Just a short distance downriver is House Rock Rapid. On our first trip, our guide called it out but didn't tell us to get good handholds or firm footing. He was more surprised than we were when it turned out to be a wild run. Afterward, looking back upstream from where we'd come, he smiled and nodded approvingly.

The Colorado River, upstream from Navajo Bridge.

"House Rock is coming back," he said, with such joy that I still hear it in my head when something gets unexpectedly better.

Anyway, looking down from Navajo Bridge, you can see a sandbar, the kind upon which downriver boatmen will make camp. You see the still-blue water—it won't turn red until the Little Colorado confluence, where that red water gradually mixes and mingles. Colorado—of course, being Spanish for "colored"—got its name for the red part.

Every time I'm here, gazing down, part of me feels a childlike belief, wish, hope, daydream: that if I dared to jump, a raft would magically appear, and I could continue on the journey. I've not tried, for which I'm both glad and sorry.

There is a way, very close by, to be in the wild romp of the Colorado River. From Lees Ferry, if you walk down a short distance from the wide tranquil fan by the boat ramp, you get to see the Colorado in its natural habitat, if you will: dancing, surging, with white-tipped standing waves sparkling a mixed message. Part of you wants to respond to the invitation to come and play; part of you knows it would be foolish, dangerous, and perhaps your last poor decision.

We haven't seen any condors, but we spy a man in a vest taking some sort of reading, who turns out to be checking for the birds as well. He confirms our sorrowful suspicion that we are out of luck. Before leaving, we check the gift shop in the visitor center, admiring the dedication to quality architecture. Sandstone carvings into the rock, allegiance to ancient tribal structures: this place appears almost organic. Quite the opposite of the cookie-cutter visitor centers of the mid-twentieth century. I have already bought Larry a mug from here that is still cherished.

I don't know how many photographs I have from here; they are probably almost identical. But I can't bring myself to leave without taking another.

"Sounds like there was more grace than grief in the passing."
—Julie, talking with Lisa after farewelling Larry for the last time.

CAMERON

Christmas Morning

Contrasting the winter of space—
motionless, stark, silent—
curiosity accelerates,
quickening the more
miles and pines fall behind us.

Come on,
            get here.

Horizon the first, best opening.

Another, the pause through the door:
gifts sparkle, color,
light dancing against glass,
home smells from the kitchen,
pressed tin the same sheen,
sense of occasion, as tinsel,
tree of life rugs weaving reminder:
we are part of something much greater
than what we might get today.

"The Land of the Mole People!"
—Lisa, on U.S. 89 north of Cameron, pre-hoodoos.

CAMERON TRADING POST

When the Cameron Trading Post opened more than a century ago, the bridge next to it spanning the Little Colorado Gorge was operational instead of picturesque. Wagons waited outside while owners bartered for Arbuckle's coffee instead of inspecting sweatshirts and dreamcatchers.

But the shadow play in the canyon beyond, the trill of canyon wrens, and the delight of tired travelers reaching sustenance are the same.

Julie and I join them. We look, with her new eyes and my recognizing ones, at the hammered tin ceilings soaring over the huge dining rooms; we walk among the glass cases filled with silver, coral, and turquoise jewelry. Then we enter the restaurant to order a meal that ends with pie, because that's what you do in northern Arizona if you know Larry Schnebly: you pay tribute by remembering when pioneers rounded off breakfast with a piece of pie, storing calories to make it through a long work-filled morning until lunch. His familiar "What kind of pie do you have?" is now beloved to us both.

Cameron Trading Post is a perpetual work in progress—at least since Joe Atkinson, kin to the original owners, took it over. What began as an empty space out back has become a courtyard to rival anything in far more verdant territory: elaborate rockwork, trellises, blooming plants, and birdsong seem contradictory to the stunning but admittedly harsh landscape on the other side of the walls. It's a true oasis in the summer heat, shade and birdsong and resplendent plants that make me wish I were single so I could have a picturesque wedding here.

The gallery this courtyard abuts is one of the aspects of Cameron Trading Post that marks it as different from many you pass in Arizona and New Mexico. Tourist driven, they generally offer carved alabaster eggs, small cedar boxes, children's bow and arrow sets, caps bright to the point of gaudiness.

Cameron has all those in the main building. You can buy earrings from the racks for under ten dollars a pair. You can also get inlaid pieces made by competent but unsigned artists. Then, if you go into the gallery, you

Inside Cameron Trading Post.

Historic bridge crossing the Little Colorado River at Cameron.

can get one-of-a-kind, rare, old, and handcrafted pieces made by the best artisans of this generation and those before.

Generally, there's at least one bus at Cameron Trading Post; sometimes the line to the restroom makes you wish you'd arrived right before it instead of after. But the dining room staff stays caught up, and stasis returns in short order.

Should you make more than a meal out of your trip and elect to spend a night, you will be surprised to find your room thoughtfully decorated, with carved wood details echoed in the design of the furniture. Thicker than expected towels, carpets, and walls seem more like a high-end lodge than a hotel at the crossroads of (very) rural Arizona.

In the evening, and again in early morning, the old bridge almost poses for photographs; a relic of design that somehow embellishes rather than detracts from the natural landscape.

And if, after you leave, you find yourself regretting not buying that piece that caught your eye, there's another convenient, if slightly out of character, option: the Cameron Trading Post website. Giving the people what they want is what keeps good trading posts busy trading posts.

"It's tough movin' west."

—Lisa, quoting Larry Schnebly's wry only response to any limitation or challenge that stems from aging.

Image of ghost aspen looking down at Navajo National Monument

HEADING NORTHEAST

DINÉTAH

lephant's Feet.

Elephant's Feet

A rock formation stands two-legged
beside the solitary highway
through Tonalea, Arizona:
mighty, resolute,
the balanced stance
selected by those prepared
to hold steady.

These pillars, reminiscent
of the forelimbs of pachyderms,
are what love can do:
almost nothing about the world
except be steady and solid.
It cannot change the landscape:
harsh, devoid of comforts;
it cannot stop the selfie interests
of passersby, pausing
only for themselves,
then hastening away at great speed.

Therefore, we must treat love
not as service station,
rest stop, or roadside attraction—
places to see only to ourselves—
nor as something
where we may unburden,
counting on it to carry us.

Love may not walk off,
but it has its own necessities
that, if ignored, can consume it
down to its unmoving feet.

"Am I sultan, or am I sultan?"
—Lisa, quoting Disney's 1992 *Aladdin* to remind us when the choice is ours.

ROAD TO DINÉTAH

I've always found it unbalanced that while the vast majority of Arizona residents live in the Valley, most of what defines Arizona touches the edges of the state. Some of those areas (Grand Canyon, Tombstone, Lake Powell) are better traveled than others. Julie and I have realized that our east and west forays are not as numerous as our north and south.

Today we traverse some new roads, out toward, then on, the Navajo Reservation. We will be Dinétah, or "among the People," in their language. Some famous but not often seen aspects of Arizona are on deck for our day.

About twenty miles past Tuba City, near Tonalea on U.S. 160, are the Elephant's Feet. Technically mid-Jurassic sandstone, they really do look like the leathery sagging ankles and feet of a massive pachyderm. I know somewhere in the area are actual dinosaur tracks, but they would require a detour, and these are far more whimsical anyway. Part of the charm of the Elephant's Feet is that they are set apart, not designated or marked with any signage or plaque. They simply stand stolid by the road as if that's where the elephant happened to stop before the rest of him or her eroded. I'm mixed about this: perhaps more people should have the pleasure of looking forward to marking this off their Arizona Life List. Perhaps it's more fun to feel like one of the in-crowd. Again, I tell Julie, "Add this to the long list of people who don't ask me what they should do." Elephant's Feet publicity is not part of my job.

I've long loved the Code Talkers Exhibit in Kayenta. Its improbable location (inside the Burger King) in no way diminishes the variety and interest of the collection, although certain materials would be disturbing to some viewers. The last time I was here, my dad recalled things he'd not thought of since World War II. I love looking at these carefully curated relics with the scent of frying and cooking on the side. It says to me, "You don't have to be one thing or another; you can be a combination." Now that we can check anything online on our computers or phones, Navajo Code Talkers are a click away, but in short, they are the largest group of Native

Julie angling for the best shot of distant Bears Ears.

language speakers who confounded the Japanese through the end of the war by using, for example, the Navajo word for "egg" for "bomb," "bird" for "plane," and "iron fish" for "submarine" in sending messages to and from the Pacific Theater. Philip Johnston, whose father had been a missionary on the Navajo Reservation, was fluent enough in the difficult language to think using it in the World War II program might just work.

Some of the signs that we are not on familiar roads are restroom signs at a travel center, in English and Navajo. More than thirty years ago as a television news reporter, I'd done a story about how state election ballots were printed in Spanish and English but not Navajo. I've also tried several times to teach myself Navajo and failed. But I recognize the multiple diacritical marks as only part of the difficulty, along with mastering glottal stops. Here, I resolve to give it one more try.

Then there's a bonus. From the parking lot at Monument Valley (more about that in its own section), we can barely see Bears Ears, which are included in a designated national monument in Utah. Julie is so excited to see part of a massive imaginary animal that she scrambles to the roof of the truck trying to obtain a better view. It reminds me of Bruce Babbitt's brief presidential campaign, when a not-yet-famous Mike McCurry watched a photographer shooting video as he walked backward up a concourse and said dryly, "I love cinema verité." Julie gets the shot.

We stay at one of the local lodges, anonymous and adequate, with a breakfast buffet that could be in most cities in America. We know, ruefully, that we could have gone to the Blue Coffee Pot for local color, but we're tired and have another long day ahead. Our final stop along the Navajo Road tour is the museum in Tuba City, with its invitation to "Explore Navajo" over the door. The architecture seems a hybrid of a hogan and a geodesic dome. Inside, it's clear top talent curated the exhibits. They are lucidly described, include history and culture, and are not stiffly treated, but they're presented in an approachable style that doesn't make a viewer from way out of town feel ignorant.

We wander and learn, again employing the informal motto to "never pass up a gift shop." It's not that we need merchandise to keep experiences, but shopping local always feels right. Straddling consumer culture and tribal heritage is well done here. It deserves support.

"If I'm laughing at myself, I know it's Divine humor."

—Julie, each time circumstance hands her planned approach an alternate route.

Guardian Head, on the way down to Betatakin in Navajo National Monument.

NAVAJO NATIONAL MONUMENT

When Walls Have Ears

You are not alone here.

Beyond the usual rummage of lizards,
history rustles on a bantering breeze
as a copse of Mormon tea
mimics the ridge's red elevation,
twin outcroppings make faces,
and curves in the creek might hiss,
except our hosts do not allow
inhospitable welcome.

Glyphs mark these facades
as though it is they, not you,
with their souls etched
by the spirits who carved out
not just a living, but a luster for life,
evident by the play of light on the leaves,
glint in the water, ghost off the aspen,
and the mime of rocks,
changing shape at every glance while
cones crackle in the agile shade
beside each ease of green.

"You'll get something out of it you didn't expect."
—Larry Schnebly, responding to an adolescent Lisa.

NAVAJO NATIONAL MONUMENT

The trail to Betatakin is long, and longer coming back out.

Julie and I have stayed the night before our hike in Kayenta to get an early start; we know the heat will make the return trip even more punishing. I've been to Navajo National Monument with my dad; in fact, one of my favorite photographs is of what I call "ghost aspen," pale skeleton winter trunks in front of what I could see of Betatakin, looking down from the rim on my previous trip.

But this time, we're goin' in.

Arriving at the visitors' center, we find you must wait for the guide and the rest of the hikers. A very knowledgeable Diné man gives us a brief orientation: take enough water, wear a hat, stay with the group. This will be a three-mile trek down to the cliff dwellings, including a steep stone staircase of almost a thousand steps. (The alternative is taking a milder incline, but it adds two miles in each direction.) We are told that only about eighty rooms remain due to rockfalls in the area, and that sandstone and wood were the materials used to build them. Betatakin means "House Built on a Ledge" in Navajo. The Hopi people call it Talastima, or "Place of the Corn Tassel." Paiute and Zuni people have also occupied this canyon, which was pretty much abandoned during a period of significant migration around AD 1300.

Our guide, who introduces himself simply as Charlie, points out many things as we walk; sadly, most of them fall out of my head before we get back to the parking lot. But that isn't his fault; it's all mine.

Julie is joyously taking in a lot of the sights on the way down enthusiastic as a dog or a child, including the point from which we can all clearly see rocks that evoke both a man's head and a lizard's head in profile.

It's already warm, and I'm drinking a lot of water. We trudge. The sun rises ever higher. It's sweaty, and frankly, for me, a bit boring. By the time we're almost to Betatakin both of us are thinking about starting back before the temperature rises any more and get permission to head back up the trail. There's really no way to get lost, and if we did stop, the group would find us.

But before we leave, we at least gaze at what we came for. As always, the enigma of who built this, who lived here, and why they left is powerful. It almost seems irreverent to converse. Those who came before deserve a respectful silence. It's wonderful this much remains. It's also tragic it was surely looted and badly treated by earlier explorers and visitors. Once we've looked our fill, we start the seven-hundred-foot ascent.

I've always loved walking downhill, and hated coming up. In fact, for years my father and I missed the chance to run Schnebly Hill Road because he wanted to ascend and I wanted to descend. (By the time we did it for his seventy-fifth birthday, he had agreed to drive the six miles up to the overlook and run back down.)

Today we definitely, inexorably, have to do both directions on foot. Other than childbirth, I don't remember anything being quite this hard. But I'm chagrined with myself: I did eight miles in forty-mile-an-hour winds at Chaco Canyon, steeper ascents in the Grand Canyon. What is wrong with me? Not enough breakfast? Getting too old? Excoriating myself, I remember an old fad called "biorhythms," which were supposed to predict days of more and less energy. Maybe they're real. What the bloody hell is my problem? I'm making it much worse hating myself.

Replenishing post-hike.

Fortunately, while I stumble and melt down, Julie stays calm and encouraging, sharing her water, and resourcefully finding shade for rests that she calls with calm authority. I'm a dazed obeying mess. I hate relying on her like this, even while I know I wouldn't mind it if roles were reversed. Pride is a terrible thing to lose.

Journeys are about more than sightseeing. They include sharing experiences and learning about ourselves and others. I learned that Julie is a wonderful guide and counselor; she remains respectful and solicitous. I'm a worse follower, wasting energy on shame and frustration. But we finally get almost to the top and take a victorious photo to mark this ignominious event. At the time, I'm resistant. Really? This experience is the last thing I want to remember. But later, I'm glad we took the photo. This is an important moment, even if not my favorite. My friend came through for me when I needed her most. That's worth a souvenir picture.

"Anywhere else, I'd say a dozen cookies is excessive.
Here, it feels like hardship rations."
—Julie, commenting on her very tasty haul from the
Jacob Lake Inn Country Store.

MONUMENT VALLEY

Between Bears Ears and Elephant's Feet

Diné creation stories explain: when the People ascended
to this Fourth World, covered in water,
everything glittered.
With directions to establish, work to be done,
play is not mentioned, but must have been present.

Anyone who has been to the beach
knows the joy of sand sculpture.
Buckets and trowels we'd never touch
in our waterless worlds back home
become coveted tools for tideside amusement.

We can all fancy ourselves Creators,
shaping castles, molding forms of friends,
perhaps even parts of ourselves,
patting layers into place
until it's time to emerge, roaring and splendid,
free of the dark, charged
to range and regain the world.

"It's possible to not believe in gravity,
but it doesn't mean it's not holding you."
—Lisa, reflecting on moments of grace.

MONUMENT VALLEY

When it comes to Monument Valley, to me one of the best parts of the trip is outside the actual Monument Valley Navajo Tribal Park boundaries. But it is as much a part of the geology and landscape as anything John Ford made famous in a film during the golden age of Western movies.

Like Elephant's Feet, it is neither part of a formal park or preserve, neither fenced nor signed. It's Agathla, a neck of rock that has outlasted the rest of the volcanic structure it was formed in. It reminds me of a snag—a dramatic, polished, twisted ponderosa pine skeleton still standing. Only this one is made of stone, one of nature's finest, and least appreciated, sculptures.

Perhaps because it is on its own, unheralded, Agathla evokes a particular reverence in me. Also, my dad, Larry, showed it to me, describing seeing it as a child during the time his father taught at the school in Dennehotso. Anything learned from him gets extra credit to me. Further, maybe

Agathla, south of Monument Valley. (Photo by Larry Schnebly.)

Monument Valley is such a sensory overload that it's like opening dozens of presents; it becomes the norm rather than a treat. Agathla stands alone, and mostly stays that way. Unlike tourists gathering like a flock of camera birds at Monument Valley, I've never seen another person taking a picture at Agathla.

Which isn't to say Monument Valley isn't amazing. On an early family vacation, my father drove the six Schneblys in the brand new 1969 Ford LTD (with an eight-track player) along the winding road across the valley floor, past one, then two, then three juxtaposed towers of sandstone, all dramatic and unique.

At some point between that trip and the next time I visited with him, my dad had gone on an educational foray on the reservation which included a traditional Diné meal of lamb stew in a Monument Valley hogan. (He remembered the stew from when his father taught at schools in the area as gristly and intense, but enjoyed the accompanying bread we associate with Navajo tacos.) When he and I returned in 2014 the road was so rutted and rough that after more than an hour we gave up and reversed course.

So when Julie and I go, it's a pleasant respite to do all the observing from one place, and at sunset.

They call it a golden hour for a reason. The gradual shift of light to a horizontal source burnishes the rock and suffuses the sky in changing tones of periwinkle to palest pink to coral and gold, sometimes infusing the rocks with what looks like inner incandescence.

Watching the light show, I think of John Wetherill, who was both one of the valley's staunchest supporters and one of its biggest nightmares. An early, indomitable explorer and trading post merchant, Wetherill embodied the best and worst of newcomers to the ancient land. He considered anything lying about to be free for use. And he wasn't alone—even huge timbers the Pueblos had used to construct Chaco Canyon's buildings were repurposed by later Navajo residents. Wetherill shared his era's interest in seemingly abandoned buildings and possessions, and its disregard for the sacred aspects of them. Were you to weigh what are now viewed as his contributions and crimes, where the scale ended up balanced would depend on your perspective.

But while Wetherill took liberties and items, he also passionately protected some sites, even writing to the National Park Service in 1909 about Monument Valley that he would "gladly look out for the ruins without

The road in front of East and West Mittens with Merrick Butte during golden hour.

pay until such a time as some regular superintendent can be appointed," lobbying for a Navajo national site to be created.

Years ago, you couldn't stay at the Monument Valley Navajo Tribal Park—hotels were back in Kayenta, about twenty-five miles away. Now the view can be seen from what is appropriately named The View: a sprawling lodge in appropriate sandstone color but disconcerting modern architecture, where visitors at least benefit the tribe as they shop, stay, dine, and take tours.

Having dozens of people all watching the sun play over the famous Mittens and other rock formations doesn't mar the event if you're after photos; though for a meditative experience it would be regrettable. Julie and I snap a few shots of each other. Then we settle down to being spectators of the somewhat passive but no less dynamic main feature: sunset on the monuments. Some moments elicit actual audible admiration, as light comes to rest just so on an abutment or slice of sandstone.

It's often said we take vacations for the photographs, and nowhere is it truer than Monument Valley. The images are perfect souvenirs. Looking at them, it's almost possible to hear the near-silence, punctuated by subdued delight, as Nature turns in yet another flawless performance for a grateful audience.

"To the degree we choose to love any living creature,
our lives are both richer and more complicated."

—Lisa, to Julie, then vice versa, at news of an animal,
friend, or family illness or struggle.

A view of Agathla, a volcanic neck south of Monument Valley.

HEADING EAST

Standin' with Augie on the Standin' Corner.

WINSLOW

A Fine Sight

Too big for a dot,
too small for a seat,
too sparse for a base,

too tended to fade,
too planted to stray,
too worn to wear out,

too real to be cliché,
too iconic to be just anywhere,
too known to be new,

too signed to miss,
too much sky for the windshield,
too much heart for the bumper.

"Sex and love are like spirituality and religion:
best together, but often apart."
—Julie, observing the obstacle course/circus/Oregon Trail redux
that is adult dating.

WINSLOW

For a town with not a lot in it, so much is here.

For many, Winslow, Arizona, is the "standin' on a corner" place in the Eagles song "Take It Easy." Winslow works it: Stitchin' on a Corner and Sleeping on a Corner are local businesses selling sewing supplies and mattresses, respectively. In addition, the city wisely designated a photo-op plaza at an intersection, with Eagles gift shops facing from two other corners and Eagles songs for background music as you pose. We will return to that.

Winslow also celebrates being on Route 66—the name was changed back to the famous freeway from Second Street about thirty years ago. Souvenirs, signs, painted street murals: you never have to wonder where you are.

To the extent that places are stages on which we play out our lives, Winslow is rich to me; my mother grew up here, I met my husband here, I hope to restore the old high school here, I've written repeatedly about La Posada here. And I got the best sound bite of my life here; more on that later.

Julie and Augie and I drive through gorgeous atmospherics from Flagstaff, wishing the Flatbed Ford Café were open for lunch but never sorry to "have to" go to La Posada. Mary Colter's gorgeously restored and most loved resort spreads out savored moments as lavish as the gift shop offerings. This is where my father realized he was falling in love with my mother (but they couldn't afford a wedding reception here, at a dollar per person, in 1953). It's where I got to watch trains rolling through outside the French doors by my bed on a trip with Larry. It's where we had a Centennial book celebration. I remember doing a story here for Channel 3 before Tina Mion and Allan Affeldt bought it and made it the crown jewel it is, and what Mary Colter said when she heard Fred Harvey was closing it after the Depression: "There is such a thing as having lived too long." I feel that way sometimes, but not today. We savor hearty lunches and sample three desserts before we walk it all off.

Augie's a good walker, past the Route 66 graphic in the street that provides the foreground for the Standin' Corner, to the gazebo in a park by the tracks. Winslow spends on entrance signs and pocket parks for 9/11 and Route 66 and the railroad. And, of course, for the Standin' Corner. We take the requisite photos ourselves, chatting with fellow pilgrims by the Glenn Frey bronze statue—and wondering who the more recent addition statue represents. I've never been here when there weren't abundant enthusiastic fellow tourists. I'm glad the song didn't instead make somewhere else famous.

Downtown looks a darn sight better than it has in earlier years, after the construction of Interstate 40 made Winslow passable and the once-robust town faded and folded one store at a time. Kenna's Corner includes a former service station; some buildings with great bones have been brought back. For every one of those there are two more waiting to be rescued. I point out the Falcon, where a mural seemed like the height of Continental dining to nine-year-old me. We also visit Mojo Coffee—the owner's father came to this country and got a little help learning English from my mother when she was a waitress for his grandfather at the Grand Café. Then his father ran the Entre here for years, so he's a third-generation restaurant entrepreneur.

La Posada.

I've never been to a tack and feed store, so Julie takes me to the one here where she got cow hay for less during her ranching life. Other than gift bags there isn't much for us today, but it's fun to see a part of her life I'd never have known existed otherwise. There are also horseshoes, not collectibles, but as footwear, singly and in packs of four, for a couple dollars. I'm charmed, and get several as gifts for my son, Rye, and brother, Linds.

Then we visit my grandparents' former home; the lovely current owner has told me I can come and dig up some of a fragile-looking but robust climbing vine my grandma planted and called silver lace. Ann ends up doing the digging, while Augie exercises a mighty will not taking on her cat. We talk about the improvements my grandpa made that she appreciates: his workmanship on shelves and doors. And I literally get to take a part of my roots when we go.

Winslow, like perhaps any small town, just needs a certain number of people who love it and are willing to work on it to bring it back. One of the best is gone; that was Tommy Thompson, the president of the Chamber of Commerce who decided to restore Route 66 to its original name and had a grand opening.

When I was interviewing him for Channel 3 in 1990, he gestured to the black-and-white sign, talking about even bigger plans.

"What else is black and white?" I wasn't keeping up, so he answered his own question, too excited to wait for me. "The space shuttle! If we could get a Route 66 sign on the space shuttle, Route 66 could go all the way to the moon! I wrote to NASA, and you know what?" He paused to savor the moment. "They haven't said no."

They haven't said no. The world maybe hasn't said a resounding yes to Winslow yet, but it hasn't said no. I'm still trying to figure out how to restore the high school.

"You can't iron with a dog."

—Lisa's working title for the dating memoir she's played with writing, referring to why women are so often disappointed that men don't respond the way women wish they did. Julie speaks for all women, and readers, when she says, "Please write that book."

HANNAGAN MEADOW

An Evening Meadow's Lark

These are wet woods, fragrant,
silent for moss underfoot.
Ferns yellow in what's left
of autumn light,
as the meadow glows gold.
Aspen, like hazel eyes on the ridge,
wait for dusk's parade of deer
bounding in
then out of the park to feed,
cloven hooves thumping against rock,
the sure sound of a gymnast
on a tumbling run—
the spring between loft and land—
though nothing's running here.
No cars, no generators,
no thrum or clatter of a peopled place,
just the breath sounds of altitude:
pounding hearts, rasping throats,
and a symphony of inner workings
trying to slow.
The calm is lush, like undergrowth,
above which conifers stretch—
bedposts above this thick cover—
into which I want to settle, nestling,
like night into the velvet grass—
like the stars into those darkening hazel eyes—
and sleep myself home
for surely this place is from dreams.

"Want to go for a walk?"
—Both of us. Anywhere. Any time of day.

HANNAGAN MEADOW

Up to now, I've merely passed Hannagan Meadow, but having heard KTVK-TV3 reporter Steve Bodinet wax rhapsodic about it, I'd long wanted to actually make it a destination instead of just scenery. Julie and I get to make that happen.

Few places in Arizona have only one purpose: visiting. Castle Hot Springs and a few ranches in southern Arizona are by themselves. But generally, when you go somewhere, you can get gas and a few groceries, mail a letter, visit some attractions. Hannagan Meadow exists purely, simply, and only for the pleasure of spending time. You can fish, and in some seasons there's snow for cross-country skiing. Somehow, there's a luxury in knowing that every minute you're there you won't get any business or errands done. You come to enjoy nature, enhanced by what human effort has created: a cozy, welcoming, quintessential lodge in the forest.

We drive through Salt River Canyon, stop for lunch in Globe, and spend some delighted time wandering the Western Drug & General Store in Springerville. (My mother and her college roommate wrote a song about two feckless boyfriends, including the line, "There's a little lake in Springerville where Malcolm and Sam are fishin' still." Up to now, that's been the sum total of my Springerville experience.) Carrying a little bit of everything the locals could want—read: heavy on camo print and outdoor supplies—with a cattle mural over the fabric section, we get Western General Store t-shirts to commemorate the experience before heading on. Julie also buys a bandanna as an homage to the cool kid from a mountain town who once asked her to dance at summer camp.

Julie's father has fondly described hearing the elk bugle at Hannagan Meadow, and how they seem to summon their strength to leap a fence with no running start. (The first time I heard that bugle it sounded to me like a cross between a whale and a dog.) My husband, Tom, was with the aforementioned Steve Bodinet at this lovely rustic lodge during long days of television newscasts there. KTVK-TV used to take huge crews on the road to showcase Arizona's wonders. I've made reservations and look forward

Cabin at Hannagan Meadow Lodge.

to staying in the Babbitt room. One of the first grocery stores I remember was the Babbitts' in Winslow, and I covered Governor Bruce Babbitt before and during his presidential campaign, before his interior secretary service.

But after carrying our bags up the stairs to our rooms (and at 9,200 feet that's no small feat) we find out mine's not made up, so I take a trip back downstairs to the puzzled desk clerk and end up going up yet another floor to the George Wiley Paul Hunt room. As a seven-time governor, he also holds a special place in my historic heart, so it's fine. (I like seeing that the lodge used both his middle names instead of just one.) We put down our bags and set out to explore.

Across the highway, the meadow itself awaits, with its picturesque broken fence. Eager as children to see somewhere we've never been, we come back to the lodge side of Highway 191 to follow a wide trail, redolent with pine and sunshine.

Every few steps reveals something remarkable: a burst of brightly illuminated red leaves backdropped by green; a baby aspen glowing a light fern shade against darker grown-up trees; a mother deer waiting for her fawn, who races toward the mom with surprisingly loud hooves on the packed earth before both disappear. Firs dominate the landscape, with some massive ponderosas adding their familiar sweet aroma. We finally reverse course, looking at all the cabins we didn't choose to stay in. We don't see another soul. Maybe they're all fishing, or the area is wide enough to let each of us feel like the only people around. Julie tells me the story of a memorable dancing camper. We wonder about small trees among large, admire the meadow again, walk near and through mud, and talk about dinner.

We were hungry before the hike, and we're ravenous now, glad to seat ourselves by the window in case there's an elk revue in the meadow at dusk. Kevin, our genial and affable server, actually sits with us while describing dinner options: ribeye and salmon win. Because they evoke such an era, I opt for cellophane-wrapped crackers from the salad bar instead of the warm bread brought on a board.

No elk appear, but about a dozen deer come picking their way delicately across the meadow while our food cooks. All the diners savor the show; even if we aren't quite city slickers, this isn't our usual evening entertainment.

Julie at Hannagan Meadow in tribute kerchief.

Once sated and replete, we go to our rooms, noting the coffee offerings in the lounge outside Julie's door. We will meet in the morning and rely on brought breakfast items; we have hundreds of miles to cover, and the dining room won't open until eight.

The room under the eaves is nicely warm from the wall heater I left on, and the bed passes the comfort test of any twenty-first-century resort. It's taken a long time, but I finally know what it's like to stay at Hannagan Meadow.

It was worth the wait.

"Think of people like zoning. Some can only do a few things with you, and others are wonderfully multiuse."

—Lisa, making sense of human relationships.

Kerchief to *Curandera*

Wherever she lived, the sick and injured followed, begging for the touch of Teresita's hand. In 1897, [she] moved to Clifton, Arizona. Local citizens soon came knocking on Teresita's door for respite from innumerable troubles. Stories circulated that she helped ease the suffering of a young Clifton boy stricken with polio.

—JAN CLEERE, "WESTERN WOMEN: BELIEVERS FLOCKED TO HEALING POWERS OF TERESITA URREA," TUCSON.COM, SEPTEMBER 19, 2016

Only yesterday, I wore a kerchief—
a summer crush
crossed the whole room
to choose me—
favored with a dance,
then with a token—

today,
a phone call from my doctor:
"fibroids—
          biopsy—
                    hysterectomy soon—"

here, just now, this news and my view
are mine tailings beside white mountains—
a sudden study in slag—
barren of potential
due to extraction—

today was supposed to be for tokens—
instead, I am a supplicant
too similar to the *curandera*
once foraging among these hills
for prayers to heal.

CLIFTON

iew from Teresita's resting place.

CLIFTON

For years Clifton was, to me, part of the miners' strike of 1983. As a brand new reporter for Channel 9 in Tucson, I went up one memorable weekend and eagerly interviewed some of the men on the picket line, as well as the spokesman from Phelps Dodge, the mining company. (The strike made national headlines when Governor Bruce Babbitt called the Department of Public Safety in for security as tensions escalated, and seemingly everyone over the age of ten had an opinion about it.) It was humbling, back then, to hear the stories of tough working conditions. Years later I interviewed people who had been children in Arizona mining towns, where the constant chemicals gave them asthma. But they'd been told by their parents to lie if asked about coughing; the mines supported the families.

Now I'm back for a much lighter reason: Julie wants to pay her respects to a healer, a historic curandera named Teresita, who was one of her favorite author's protagonists and now lies, reportedly, in an unmarked grave in the Clifton Cemetery. We've come through Morenci, one of Arizona's sets of linked towns. Clifton-Morenci, Dewey-Humboldt, and Pinetop-Lakeside are always mentioned in lockstep. I was told KTVK-TV news director Phil Alvidrez had been the first to break an invisible barrier by being from Clifton and dating a Morenci girl. Or vice versa. As years pass, our brains bury old stories under new ones.

Morenci is the only place I know that you actually drive through the copper mining arena and operation. Tailings are the growing piles of unused ore. This is the opposite of that: deepening crevasses and basins where copper (and everything else) has been removed in open-pit mining. A curving road takes you down, down, to where vehicles far below had moments before seemed miniature. The striated colors and acidic scent accompany you through town. The photo I'll always most wish I had taken was of a man, alone on a horse in an empty field on the outskirts, looking at his phone. Where centuries collide.

Today, rain gives Clifton an overlay of desolation, like an Edward Hopper painting where everyone is, or feels, alone. If geographic features are related, like one monadnock to another, so are copper towns: main streets with fading commerce, a few picturesque buildings, big houses higher in the hills than the workers' cottages. Often the parking on the main street

Clifton depot.

is diagonal. Clifton has a lovely old train station, and the tracks seem to go right through the center of town.

We talk about how different our lives would have been being born here; what accident of birth put us in Arizona's big cities? Would our worldviews have been the same, or radically altered? I feel restless and a little sad looking at houses here, but I am also humbly reminded of a Holbrook couple who would go to Hawaii every year, then return to watch the sun set from their backyard and say, "Now, this is paradise." Maybe I'm just not meeting the people who feel that way here. Because of the rain, I don't think we see a single person outside a vehicle. And the town isn't very big.

We marvel at how far out the cemetery is: several miles away from the living, but the location does give its residents (and their visitors) a spectacular view. Was there some sort of epidemic that made people think burial shouldn't be closer in? There's no one to ask. We brave the rain, picking our way down a steep unpaved path to get closer to unmarked plots, passing an apparent gathering of stone cherubs, and two obelisks of stacked mineral rock: one still copper and the other now verdigris to turquoise shades. As expected, Teresita's unmarked grave protects her anonymity. We talk about how hard it must have been, as the 1800s rolled into the

1900s, to be an independent woman with a career, and a potentially suspiciously regarded one at that. We opine that white men with power could have feared love potions or assisted abortions.

Colors of the stones and setting range from bleak to fading in the thick rain. To leave, we drive on a funny little road under a railroad bridge and head south. Since we haven't spoken to a soul during our time here, we can't gauge hospitality or happiness levels among the residents. Maybe it would be a very different experience if the sun and people were out.

I hope to always have a mug that I paid four dollars for in 1983 that reads, "Support the Copper Strikers." I leave with a lingering feeling of not having done enough.

"The time to laugh is whenever you can."

—Lisa, quoting Fiddler from *Roots.* One of the biggest perks of this friendship is getting to giggle at the inappropriate with impunity.

DUNCAN

owntown Duncan streetscape.

I Am a Town

Adapted from the song of the same title by Mary Chapin Carpenter

I am old Americana, an antique road trip prize,
the quiet of parade grounds after everyone's inside,
I'm supply to county fairgrounds when the beer tent's out of ice,
I am soda-fountain-frothy to those who've just arrived.

I'm the ride on bareback horses, greeting drive-bys with a wave,
I'm the sound of pausing footsteps as they'd echo on the planks,
I am dedicated markers
to people come and gone,
rarely noticed by those passing
as Life keeps urging on.

I'm drawn from simple lines, I face the world one-sided,
you're from here or you're not, but welcome will be timeless.

I am Arizona-born, New Mexi-can, why can't we?
I may be a mere dot on maps, but, seen, you won't mistake me,
I'm a mug of conversation, I'm the quench of lunch iced tea,
I'm the daily special signboard
spelling out a joke for free.

I am postcard rural-living, just the size of stamps,
I am sliding onto vinyl chairs, seat wet from the damp,
I am rolling down my window, hand raised from the wheel,
smile as soft as seed pods, tough as railroad steel.

I am a town,
homebound.

"I'd better drive."

—Julie, when a curvy road approaches.

—Lisa, after Julie drives, yet manages to get carsick on curves anyway.

DUNCAN

Small towns in Arizona have some similarities, but each is significant in its own way.

They may take you back to the Victorian era, the Wild West, or the heyday of King Copper.

Duncan takes you back to 1963.

It's as if a set designer with an unlimited budget swept through to create the feeling of what a small rural town would be when the Beatles were about to become famous, a Buick Rivera cost three thousand dollars, and a magazine ad showed a woman with a fake black eye who would rather fight than switch cigarette brands. It's pitch-perfect.

Bakery courtyard with mural.

Just five miles from our border with New Mexico, Duncan began as a way station for ore trains. Now it uses its anachronistic vibe to charm tourists (and some new residents).

Julie and I notice right off that, amazingly, there are no franchises on the main streets. The Simpson Motel surely looks much like it has since it opened a century ago (though it now offers vegan breakfasts); next to it the Bank of Duncan is housed in a creamy brick building from 1908.

We marvel at the lush flower gardens and brick work around the traditional round black four-sided clock outside the Henrie Brothers Bakery.

We read the rough wooden sign outside the Stage Stop Mini Mart & Liquor Store showing gas prices a good half-dollar lower than anywhere else we've been. Seeing "pellets on sale" makes us conclude that if you have to wonder what type of pellets, you aren't the target audience.

No one passes us on the street, and I'm glad, because if they didn't leave a whiff of Aqua Velva or Brut, I would be disappointed.

Hilda's Kitchen and Meat Market puts a hat on the whole experience. Painted wooden shelves hold the most unfamiliar products I've ever seen: brands I don't recognize, with labels that look like they were lifted from a Golden Book I read as a child. If I didn't see the tall narrow cardboard box holding ice cream cones with red-headed kids on the side, I still think I did.

I had told Julie about visiting here a decade earlier with Lar and eating at a restaurant with walls of unpainted particle board and tables covered in cowhide-print vinyl. I remember marveling at our meal of two tostadas with rice, beans, chips, and salsa costing less than a ten-spot for two. The restaurant, which turns out to be called the Ranch House, is right where my dead reckoning leads, across from a church that was surely put in place by a crane that lifted it out of Mayberry. Once inside the diner, we see progress has come to Duncan after all: the walls have been painted a terra cotta hue. But the table of regulars that goes quiet when we walk in to assess us as tourists shows the residents are exactly as hoped. Men with beards, overalls, plaid shirts, and twang in their words josh each other. We smile.

Prices have risen a little, we see after choosing a patio table. A server is sweeping recent rain from flagstones while carrying on a desultory conversation with a young man clearly besotted with her. Beyond the patio wall, fields stretch out as far as the eye can see. I'm starting to wonder if I would really miss my friends that much after relocating to this bucolic burg.

Finishing lunch, we walk back to our vehicle, picturing the children who will presumably get out of school in a few hours. Surely their t-shirts would have stripes instead of logos. They would play leapfrog instead of computer games, and climb around the rustic old truck, surely older than I am, parked outside a service station.

We chat with a few folks inside a storefront that lets hobbyists and artists sell their wares, with brochures extolling the virtues of Duncan. The residents have all came by choice from bigger towns, and they all love their friendly neighbors. Julie and I opine as we leave that since the world has learned how easy it is to work remotely, Duncan has a shot at becoming a more robust metropolis by offering a nostalgically simple set, at least, for lifestyle. We hope the people who move here are smart enough to keep most of it as it is.

"I think the angels are throwing elbows."

—Julie's explanation for sudden turnarounds, moments of grace, and other blessings coming out of nowhere.

Shrine outside Tombstone.

HEADING SOUTHEAST

Veils of mountains falling away from U.S. 491 (formerly U.S. 666).

VISTAS AND SIGNS

Signs and Red Flags

Slow,
Snowmobile trailhead,
Bighorn sheep crossing,
Vista, Right—Do Not Pass—
Winding Road, 35 mph,
RV Pullout, Clifton 50,
Winding Road, 25 mph
Winding Road, 15 mph
Speed Reduced Ahead,
Winding Road, 10 mph,
Morenci, Private Property, Mine,
No Trespassing,
Clifton, Do Not Enter When Flooded,
Turn Around Don't Drown,
Duncan City Limits,
Hilda's Meats, Country Chic,
Visitor's Center Welcome,
Ranch House Restaurant,
Chili Dogs!
"I'm so busy I don't know
if I lost a horse or found a rope."
Hotel Duncan, F*$k Biden
STOP.

Old West Highway Left.

VISTAS

We may travel together, but each of us takes our own journey.

Perhaps because both Julie and I rarely see eastern Arizona, we are even more attuned to novel and unfamiliar aspects of it. She keys in on signs: these are not like those around the valley. I'm reminded of a great sign from Arizona's West Coast: Coffee Ern's. But for me, this road is about the vistas.

A major part of Arizona scenery is sky. My father has long been an observer and appreciator of our vast views. Sometimes in open space you get a plethora of types of clouds all in one gaze: wispy virga falling far away from faint gray, with towering puffs of snowy cumulus piling ever higher close by, and various mares' tails of nimbus that are pulled in the wake of the wind in between. Larry would nod approvingly, and say simply, "atmospherics," with deep satisfaction, almost like saying the first name of a beloved friend.

The day we drive from Hannagan Meadow to Clifton, and later from Fort Bowie to Willcox, we get more atmospherics per mile than probably any other day I remember. I tell Julie I was very relieved when I finally got to Montana a few years ago and discovered that what I had long suspected was true: their skies are no bigger than ours. We just don't talk about them on our license plates.

Some places always offer a great view: heading south on Interstate 17 around the Oak Creek exit, where veils of mountains fall away like pages in a book across the southern sky; coming east across U.S. 89 from Jacob Lake toward Marble Canyon, where the Vermilion Cliffs show up knife-edge sharp against open land. I had not remembered that coming down U.S. 491 (formerly the famous 666) skirting the edge of New Mexico is another. You see this last one for a very long time because you must drive so slowly.

I've been on this road only three times in my life, and each of the other two times signaled the end of a romance. I think long days in a car punctuated by stretches of nothing much to do in a rural setting tested the relationships and found them wanting. So the drive on that road from Greer to Tucson was in some ways the funeral procession for two relationships. Probably both travel companions were relieved, as I guess I was. But I tell Julie that Tom and I had been in love for twenty years before I felt completely safe going to Greer with him.

Today, of course, Julie and I have no such concerns: we have jogged over rough roads, been unsure of directions, found ourselves facing a much longer day due to lack of lodging than we'd planned, and never turned on one another. The only challenges are nausea and restlessness, creeping and weaving down the formidable spine of the White Mountains.

But we persevere, so we succeed. Through Duncan, on to Fort Bowie, and then into an encore of wild and spectacular atmospherics.

This storm unleashes true fury on the land, coming not as a friendly, welcoming, nourishing rainfall but as a conqueror. Streams spring up on each side of the road with standing water on the asphalt, so fast does the sky release the water. Driving gingerly, not because of bad road, but in fear of hydroplaning, we are at least not too nervous to appreciate the utterly transformed scenery we behold. In this case the unremarkable desert is so diminished by the size and majesty of the clouds that we barely notice the land. So many shades of gray: dove and ash deepening to charcoal and something more menacing.

Virga on I-10, east of Willcox.

We agree this is one more demonstration that few things are ever truly good or bad. Road conditions: hazardous. The view: matchless. All in all in all, as Tom says and as Julie and I have added to our lexicon, we count ourselves fortunate to be able to drive these roads and witness these fleeting and magnificent versions of Arizona skies.

"Won't it be interesting to see what happens?"

—Lisa, quoting her mother's line that frustrated her heartbroken adolescent self and became truer with each passing year.

FORT BOWIE

emaining armory wall.

Rough Translation

When the past is foreign country
I would like a new translation—
emphasizing nuance—not stated so bluntly.

When cool facts contrast, reasoning storms sultry.
Where is truth to stand on, or any foundation,
when the past is foreign country?

When bias lacquers, making tales seem comely,
where is right perspective, just the cant for a collation
emphasizing nuance—not stated so bluntly?

If lives lived are fragile, how to do less fumbling,
damage less understanding, achieve true restoration,
when the past is foreign country?

We have drop-in understandings—often hurried—stumbly—
at a pace too breathless for any full narration
emphasizing nuance. To state as much so bluntly:

we enter places past as if we're shopping sundries
in markets stocked today, the present in presentation,
when the past is foreign country.

How to avoid the imports—find real reliquary—
gems in garbled histories claiming authentication,
emphasizing nuance, as their packaging says bluntly?

We mean no imposition—we wish to visit humbly—
inflicting no more trespass on a ravaged nation.
When the past is foreign country,
we must emphasize its nuance, if I do say so bluntly.

"Hey, a shrine! Want to stop?"
—Julie. A lot.

FORT BOWIE

If adventure is defined as not knowing what is going to happen, visiting Fort Bowie was going to be a big one.

Julie and I dithered through the entire drive as to whether we should visit this historic site in Arizona's southeast corner. The weather forecast had opened with a storm warning, then that was called and raised to severe weather. But we're this close, we say; Fort Bowie is literally on the way to nowhere. When would we be back here? I had been here with Larry, who had waxed rhapsodic for years, and it was one of the most powerful places I'd seen, only moments from history.

But on the other hand, it's a mile-and-a-half hike. Possibly in pounding rain or even hail? Then again, it's such an amazing place. I relive in description the trip with my dad. Julie and I both hold him in such high esteem, and he pronounced it worthy of seeing. Also, being in a place few people come leaves the past more intact; the air hasn't been rebreathed much. (I sometimes swear that completely changes the experience, making history less diluted, less diffused.) Seeing the tree that was here when Cochise cut himself out of his tent during the Bascom Affair puts us one degree of separation from him; standing where the Butterfield Stage came through, we are almost able to hear the creak of harness and pounding of hooves; watching water come up in the same spring Apaches, then cavalry used are powerful draws. But I'm dicey, divided.

Julie finally calls it: we're going. We park in the lot where only one other vehicle indicates someone is as brave or stupid as we are. We start the trek, watching clouds with alternating nervousness and confidence. The National Park Service has improved signage in the past ten years; we aren't wondering where the trail leads, and Cochise's captivity site has better interpretive language. Which isn't the point: to merely be where it occurred blows me away all over again.

But we don't linger; primeval clouds are building ahead of us. We pick up our already-impressive pace, finally sighting the flagpole and walls that indicate where the fort was. And the entire place is mostly past tense: I

(Almost) all that remains: cannon and eroding adobe.

remember hearing and we've read online about the icehouse to provide cold treats, the Victorian mansion the commanding officer went home to each evening. I'm looking forward to the visitor center again, and also hoping we make it there before the skies open.

We do, but we don't: when we arrive, puffing and relieved, we find out it's closed today. How did we miss this detail in everything we read? The view from the wraparound porch is commanding. We try to think ourselves back in time and see very little changed; if anything, things are more primitive now, as the barracks and most other buildings are being reabsorbed into the land. The armory is a safe distance away; I grab a photo as we pass. And we walk through the cemetery, with its mostly unmarked residents.

Then Julie's phone issues one more dire storm warning, and the brooding threatening darkening sky backs up the claim. We leave fast.

If we were efficient hiking in, now we're frightened and even faster. We watch lighting increase in aggressiveness, trying to spot trees that'll make us not the highest point on the landscape for a stray bolt to strike. So far, it's still worth coming, but we both sense that could quickly change.

Almost running, we crest the wash we came across between us and the parking lot and arrive just as the skies open.

Skilled criminals getting on a taxiing jet as it picks up speed on the runway couldn't have made a more dramatic exit or cut it closer. Hail is already collecting in trenches on both sides of the road. This is a rainstorm of biblical proportions, and we are smart enough to realize we've been way luckier than we deserved to be. And we saw Fort Bowie.

While a more leisurely visit with less pressure to get back would have been pleasant, in a way we saw everything that mattered. We saw the incongruity of a fort ever being out here at all. Yes, it made sense at the time with the stage route and Apaches—we can see why the U.S. Army chose the site. But . . . it's just so very far away from anything today that it's almost like it exists in another time plane—one where progress unfolded differently than in the world we're used to.

Most areas this remote weren't formerly more developed. Progress and population usually move forward instead of fading. That's part of Fort Bowie's appeal. It was, and now it's not, and nothing replaced it. Almost no one comes. It's not only at the end of a road, but it's past the end of a road, and an empty one at that if you don't count the tent location and the spring. Fort Bowie shares its stories with the few of us who believe in seeing not just the landmarks that everyone said "Oh, you have to see" about. It's for the people who really love every phase of Arizona history.

Driving carefully, we agree that the intensity and threat of things going very badly gave a flavor to the expedition it would have lacked on a pleasant day. It was a fitting state for a place so unsupportive of a comfortable life. And we didn't have to deal with wool uniforms or unstable munitions. Unpredictable weather in an uncertain wilderness with a happy ending makes for a very good day.

"Atmospherics."

—Larry Schnebly, viewing skies as if seeing an old friend.

—Lisa, often, and several times today.

Downtown Douglas.

DOUGLAS

Corresponding Lines[*]

<table>
<tr><td>A town lives by growing—</td><td>passed what's past, to further futures—</td></tr>
<tr><td>not by siding against country,</td><td>not stopping for tired disputes with no good side—</td></tr>
<tr><td>countryside is beyond the town—</td><td>sustaining trade is Main Street,</td></tr>
<tr><td>bustling as gateway</td><td>a welcome sign</td></tr>
<tr><td>less concerned for boundaries than</td><td>recognizing people are ever at a crossroads</td></tr>
<tr><td>lending itself to those who reach them,</td><td>wherever they've been, along a border's stretch.</td></tr>
</table>

* This poem, a contrapuntal, may be read in columns, up to down, then left to right, or in rows, left to right, then up to down. Much like border issues, understanding depends on preference and perspective.

"I think that's like asking what pictures you're going to take when you get to Belgium."
—Lisa, suggesting we try not to plan too far ahead.

DOUGLAS

Some of us remember long summer afternoons, which we had pictured during the school year as endless swimming and popsicles, instead of ending up bored, with drawn-out complaints of "There's nothing to do . . ."

I also recall a family celebration in a private dining room at an elegant restaurant for my dad's eightieth birthday being curiously flat; everyone wanting it to be festive and memorable, and no one knowing the alchemy that would lift it from doldrums. Like a becalmed ship, sometimes you can't bring the wind.

So it was in Douglas. I guess most places we visit at least held the promise of a meal. But this was a midafternoon visit to a place Julie wanted to see for an admittedly sober purpose: to find out how chain link fences between houses in formerly unified neighborhoods affected the vibe of this border town.

I'd been here, back when the border was casual and crossable, to do interviews with people who saw family members down the street, whether in Agua Prieta (AP, they called it) or Douglas with equal ease. All of them went to AP doctors, then got library books in Douglas.

This was in part because until the combined effects of the Hidalgo Treaty and Gadsden Purchase in the mid-1800s, Arizona was in Mexico, and residents of the area weren't terribly thrown by a technical change in ownership. One of legendary rancher John Slaughter's men built a house straddling the border so he could be polygamous, ushering "extra" wives into "Mexico" if the law came calling.

This is not to say things were always sunny.

I remember former (and only Hispanic) governor Raúl Castro telling a story of coming to one these picturesque parks in Douglas as a little boy to see then-governor George W. P. Hunt give a stump speech. Castro says he was only there for the free food, but Hunt caught sight of him near the edge of the gazebo from which he spoke.

Staircase in the Gadsden Hotel where Pancho Villa rode his horse.

"We're the land of opportunity! This little brown boy here could be governor someday," Castro remembers Hunt saying. Such is the stuff of legend. But Castro also talked of walking the miles to school as the bus rolled by carrying white students.

Today, the nearby smokestacks indicate another less salubrious element of Douglas history. Older residents describe their fathers coming across the Mexican border to work in mines and smelters, literally walking through a shower of insecticide so they didn't bring anything into this country with them. Their children were told to lie if anyone asked if the smelter smoke made them cough. Pollution paled compared to losing their jobs. I came back to do television stories about mines closing and hearings about smelter pollution, all part of the past now. But fewer jobs mean fewer residents and emptier businesses.

And rules, regulations, conditions, and controversy gradually increased the barriers between two countries.

We easily find a parking place. Douglas shares many qualities with other small Arizona towns: a few cars parked on downtown streets in front of shuttered businesses, with train tracks and the small parks harking back to a more social and gracious time.

Julie wants to see up close how increased border fencing has affected the local population. Even beholding the multiple coils of razor wire atop chain link fencing is uncomfortable. It's such a clear denunciation of the old ways. Houses that used to let neighbors chat face to face are now either Them or Us. It's unpleasant, and saddening, and neither of us has any good ideas about how to believe in a brighter future or a return to the old ways.

We drive, looking for a place to park in order to observe the vaunted razor wire with lives unspooling on both sides. It's elusive but we finally edge in. Not a soul is in sight. And it stays that way.

Douglas still exists by the border, growing smaller and quieter like some people do as they age. The best vestige of better days is like an elderly woman proudly wearing her too-large engagement diamond: the Gadsden Hotel still stands proud. Gleaming with gilt and gold in the light through stained glass windows, the lobby impresses even a casual visitor. They just don't build them like this anymore.

I'm always delighted to revisit the sweeping staircase in the Gadsden's lobby, where Pancho Villa supposedly rode his horse up to see the view from the mezzanine. We admire the artisanship as our steps echo on the polished floor. Without throngs of visitors, the Gadsden still reminds that human time isn't all there is. Places survive eras better than people. Maybe Douglas is in a slump, not at an end. We will come back to see sometime.

Lar always opined that the balance of nature wasn't stasis: it was flood, drought, fire, storm. And that the "good old days" included no in vitro surgery, phones that didn't leave the walls, and polio. In other words, what you're seeing isn't the whole story. You're somewhere on the spectrum of a slowly swinging pendulum.

"Put in some of that magazine s—t."
—Lisa, quoting assistant television news director
Dennis O'Neill's advice as she and Julie discussed
Julie's possible essay content.

TOMBSTONE

att Earp walked here . . . a corner in Tombstone.

Dusty Roses

"The World's Largest Rose Tree" is housed at the
Rose Tree Museum in Tombstone, AZ.
—ROSE TREE MUSEUM WEBSITE

Mary Katherine Horony Cummings
sounds rosy, but her life was dusty at best:
an immigrant whose parents died,
then a foster child, runaway,
sporting woman, and consort
to a dentist slash notorious gunslinger.

Known as Big Nose Kate,
she lived to ninety years old
during a time when dying
implied dying young.
Not for her to succumb to illness,
or hard and lawless living—
the Western way of life—
she, like this banksia cutting, grew wildly
past the confines of a cultured name.

When the notion of quitting
is more lethal than gunfire,
blooming means cultivating grit,
and thorn, to repel giving up.

"I still got one good arm to hold you with."
—Lisa, quoting a line from *Tombstone,* when it's time to just make do.

TOMBSTONE

To visit Tombstone successfully, I have to remind myself that it's the sizzle as much as the steak that we seek. When I was about ten a family trip to Tombstone included seeing the famous Boot Hill headstone: "Here Lies Lester Moore, four slugs from a .44, no Les no more."

But then back home, I saw an old black-and-white photo of my dad as a young man reading the same inscription—but on a different stone in a different spot. I was devastated: what to do if you can't trust your own eyes that you're looking at history?

Over decades I've softened this view. Tombstone is a romp through what we want the Wild West to have been. If "there's facts, and then there's truth," Tombstone is all about the story touching a legend. It amuses me to think that if it had been named Goose Flat for the ground it's on rather than Tombstone, probably the whole shootout at the OK Corral (or near it, or not) would have faded into obscurity.

Julie and I hurl ourselves into the spirit, parking in a dusty lot and walking to the town center, where each corner beckons us to indulge in some segment of Tombstone's colorful past right here in the present. At an intersection you can see a Stetson storefront, the Longhorn Saloon, and a sure-as-shootin' stagecoach.

We want lunch, and make a pilgrimage to the Crystal Palace, where we read that right on these very wooden floorboards, the honest-to-goodness boots of Virgil Earp, Wyatt's older brother, once trod. His office was upstairs. Also, Sheriff John Behan's.

My most enduring version of *Tombstone* is the 1993 movie with Val Kilmer, Kurt Russell, Sam Elliott, and Powers Boothe. Because I love Sam, I love the real Virgil, and despite my somewhat jaded reaction to Tombstone, I'm also a little reverent to know my bootsteps are tracing his.

Inside, an old photo of the ornate bar with its curved mirrors lets me re-create the scene in real time. This is what Tombstone is about: Picture Yourself Here.

We literally picture ourselves, indulging after lunch in the fantasy of being sepia-toned subjects, if not actually for C. S. Fly, for a modern-day substitute. Because we're twenty-first-century women, we opt for the cattle-drover look rather than saloon girls, although Julie does a bonus round to have both. It's silly and wonderful, like hurtling yourself into the spirit of trick-or-treating.

Back on the street, we visit the World's Largest Rose, a banksia with branches resting on wooden supports, where I buy cuttings for my brother and myself. After all, this rose tree was trading carbon dioxide and oxygen with the Earp brothers and the notorious Cowboys gang members. Believing is fun.

It's amusing and appropriate that an attraction has been added, like Disneyland. "Hey, look—new history!" Now you can see where we're told Doc Holliday's girlfriend, Big Nose Kate, was watching the famous gunfight. Part of me huffs silently that if that were true, it would have been known before now. Another part shrugs, and thinks, "Well, could be." So we visit the room. And the OK Corral.

It's fun to remember that a few years ago, pencil-scribbled sheets with a firsthand account of the shootout were found abandoned in the Cochise County Courthouse when someone went through a drawer. I guess history can be new.

We come here to feel. We want to absorb some sense of what it was like to watch the Earps and Cowboys exchange about thirty gunshots in about as many breathless seconds. We want to walk where the jingle of outlaw spurs seems just out of hearing. We want to connect ourselves to a grand legend of the Old West that the New West has made plenty of room for. Now Julie and I are part of it as well.

"True Arizona women have a fierce femininity."

—Lisa. 'Nuff said.

We eschew saloon girl costumes to be fierce Arizona women.

Moon over Bisbee.

BISBEE

True Colors

A painted lady might say
it takes courage to be colorful—
to wear weathered well
while facing into change—
verdigris unconcerned
with any patina,
because of trust in one's own
mettle.

"Every time money is exchanged for goods or services someone owns your ass."
—Lisa, quoting her brother Linds.

BISBEE

Every trip to Bisbee is full of ups and downs. Steep streets and actual stairs are part of your journey if you travel more than a few steps in any direction. In most cities you absorb more by walking than driving. To that end, Julie and I leave the car parked when we go in search of ground coffee for our hotel suite, as well as local color.

There's an art deco vibe to Bisbee—from the ornamental border on what was the Phelps Dodge Mercantile when company stores were a thing to the sculpture that is literally a copper miner. A miner, and copper. The

The matchless Virile Man statue.

plaque reads, "Dedicated to those virile men, the copper miners." They just don't write 'em like that anymore.

From our headquarters at the Carrick Hotel's charming French-doored suite, we're given directions to a market—a good puffing trip uphill. Then back downhill for a stroll through a tourist shop where an employee calls to keep another location open so we can get a certain turquoise ring. Then, a great Mexican dinner, and even once inside, more steps up and down. After that, up to our street, then up again three flights to our room.

Bisbee is kin to Jerome: each a mining town of a certain age scrabbling to maintain a foothold on steep slopes. But it's gentler and wider than its cousin, with entire neighborhoods linked together by cement stairs. Even if you didn't know it's an artists' community, you'd realize it quickly: pretty much anything that doesn't move is decorated, embellished, tiled, painted, or all of the above. The quirky charm never stops. People appear to live here by choice, which makes them genial and expansive to visitors. (Or the morose ones don't interface with the public, which is fine too.)

While the Copper Queen Hotel surely has a leftover spirit or two, and more than a century of hell-raisin' Saturday nights along Brewery Gulch must have meant a few hapless souls didn't wake up on Sunday, this isn't a place of oppressive ghost presences. We woke up from unhaunted dreams and never felt cold stares on cold stairs. In fact, we left with feelings of genuine warmth from each person with whom we'd interacted.

It's a lovely stroll from downtown out to the Bisbee Breakfast Club in the morning, which cheerfully contributes more kitsch to the landscape, inside and out. We are charmed by old cars by older gas pumps and a gum machine inside.

On the walk back past Lavender Pit and rough leftover hillsides, we talk: about how being raised with privilege beats the alternatives but carries its own challenges as well. Walks, even with longtime friends, sometimes create a zone for candor and more confidences. Add that to the long list of reasons to take road trips that include foot trips.

All this and picturesque to boot. Bisbee.

"Do what's best for you."

—Lisa, quoting Ray Lindstrom when Julie contemplated a morning step workout. (Julie opted to join Lisa on her walk of more gradual grades —and breakfast.)

Racetrack gate in Sonoita.

HEADING SOUTH

Gate at Santa Cruz County Fairgrounds, where Julie competed.

SONOITA

Running Circles

Staring at an empty track,
gates moaning, hinges stuck,
paint peeling from the aging stands,
the finish is also a forgotten start
for legends, legacies
coming from behind:
a horse who couldn't race,
and a boy who rode for his grandfather,
a chicken-farmer-turned-cattle-rancher.

That horse went on
to sire and grandsire champions
of reining, roping, and cutting:
no good for ovals, though they ran circles
around anything else in equine sports.

That boy would eventually train
two Triple Crown–winning horses.
One of only two men in history to do so.

When we begin anything,
it's easy to feel we're going in circles,
never getting anywhere,
until we're stronger for them,
others asking where we came from,
and how we got so far.

"And . . . whoa."
—Julie, while slowing to a halt, no matter the kind of horsepower involved.

SONOITA

We are all constantly surrounded by worlds we know not of.

Sonoita was one of those for me.

Julie has many layers of memories there from competing in horse shows and was eager to revisit the scene of adolescent experiences. I had been to the Sonoita Vineyard and remembered hearing that scenes from *Oklahoma!* had been filmed in those great hazy green rolling hills under infinite skies (They had to transplant a peach orchard to do it). But I came as a newcomer to fairgrounds that she returned to as an old friend.

This is sure gorgeous country, was my first thought when we got out of the vehicle. And second, as happens in rare places, human contributions to the landscape enhance rather than detract from photos. The rustic gate and barbed wire framing the view and the empty grandstand diminished by the wideness of the sky added visual grace notes.

When we heard a motor and saw a man coming slowly around the track in some sort of massive red tractor or grader, we decided to introduce ourselves.

Jimmy Lewis was wonderful.

He told us about how Bob Baffert had jockeyed there as a boy, and how Jimmy's grandfather, Blain, had held the first race ever right there at Santa Cruz Fairgrounds, where we stood, and was even better known for training Parker's Trouble. Julie was properly impressed; I had to be told Parker's Trouble was such a famous quarter horse that he's buried there on the grounds and people come to pay tribute to his memory.

Jimmy and Julie talked about the years of events she had attended there, and others he remembered for various reasons. He took us over to see the final resting place of Parker's Trouble. Other quarter horses peered out of white-painted stalls at us. I felt a familiar sense that I often experienced as a reporter: I'm visiting someone else's world, where the traditions, norms, and surroundings are vastly different from my day-to-day experiences. Jimmy speaks the language of these skies, can probably tell which way weather is heading. He knows when certain birds will come, and about the quality of hay, and how smooth a track needs to be—a thousand things he doesn't even realize he knows, so deeply are they entrenched in his mind.

Julie and Jimmy Lewis chat about famous quarter horses.

I, who have barely sat on a horse, see very tall glossy animals with unreadable faces where he sees friends—and maybe a few who for whatever reason aren't as close. Julie, as I know her, lives in my world but speaks the lingua franca and talks about sires and hands and races easily. I see for the first time the little girl who came down with her mother and got nervous before events and had ice cream afterward, when staying in hotels was a novelty we've become inured to as adults.

Right then I wanted nothing more than to come to the next event held there. I want to see the grandstands filled with spectators wearing bigger belt buckles and cowboy hats than I usually see. I want to hear that white horn blare "The Star-Spangled Banner" and see a young woman riding the circle of the track holding an American flag that ripples in the sun. I want to smell popcorn and hot dogs and dust kicked up by all the boots. I also suspect after we've been back home a day or two, that desire will fade, the way I get over wanting a tall, pointed hat with a gauzy veil at the Renaissance Festival, or wanting to buy yet another shady picture hat on every summer vacation. I hope I retain enough of this feeling to return.

"When I was growing up, and here at a horse show . . ."

—Julie, in Flagstaff, Safford, Douglas, Tucson, and Sonoita.

Velvet Elvis interior.

PATAGONIA

You Are Here

Some places make it clear
you can be nowhere else.
Standing on the North Rim,
vastness above and below,
is as unmistakable
as being beneath the reach
of a saguaro's open arms.

Other places
could be anywhere else:
big box parking lots,
stucco subdivisions
ubiquitous
as mayo on sandwiches.

But this place
could be somewhere
Lost Time lives:
few corners on quiet streets,
stories branching, leafing
from the stretch
of the trees in the square,
asking where have I been
that I have never
been here before.

"If I don't know what to do, I need more information."
—Lisa, helping Julie suss out a conundrum. Often.

PATAGONIA

Sometimes you travel wide, and other times deep. Patagonia is a very small footprint, but we feel immersed. Until Julie and I returned here, I had it in only two isolated memories. One was stopping with my high school boyfriend early in the morning on the way to the nearby lake, so hungry that a delivery man took pity on us and gave us two free honey buns. (The worst sunburn of my life followed at that lake.) The other was a ten p.m. live shot for a Channel 3 road trip series, when a proprietor who had kindly stayed open to be part of our story sold my husband Tom beautiful earrings of silver and turquoise crosses for me that I'd admired and that he went back to buy.

The genial lunchtime regulars at Velvet Elvis smile for the camera.

So this is trip 3 for me. Even in midsummer, the four-thousand-foot elevation gives us a sense of cool breezes. While some visit to see hummingbirds in nearby canyons, fewer than a thousand souls live in the metropolitan area. If you're here, it's on purpose. It's a town in miniature, with several tree-lined streets in both directions and some tourist-based commerce. Patagonia doesn't offer many remarkable reasons to visit, but the one it has attracts international attention.

Thanks to media, the Velvet Elvis has a circle of devotees far more widespread than most local restaurants can boast. The passion and brainchild of Cecilia San Miguel, this Italian eating establishment is named as a homage to paintings on velvet so prevalent across the border.

The Sonoran flavor remains strong throughout, starting in the patio yard with wrought iron and a shrine for a cherub statue. The rich hues throughout almost feel like all the walls should be dripping, so shiny and deep are they, and while the rooms evoke missions, San Miguel de Allende, and any good thing you associate with such decor, the place doesn't take itself at all seriously.

Based on our visit, neither do the guests. We are sharing a room with an uproariously happy table of regulars whose laughter draws us over. They welcome a photograph and the rights to use it without caring if their names are ever read.

The menu delivers the promised Italian offerings: calzones, strombolis, and pizza, oh my! Names like "Cara Mia with white sauce," "The Good, the Bad and the Ugly," "El Sassy," and "Southwest Diva" attest to the creative pulse of the place.

Julie and I can't stay at our table after ordering; we have to prowl the place end to end and take everything in. Velvet Elvis is filled with Things We Wouldn't Think Of. For instance, outlines of tiny desert creatures inlaid in bright stones in the cement floor make crossing the room a whimsical adventure. It's like both the inner child and adult are catered to.

Above those, everything is saturated with jewel tones. Scarves and skirts flutter, a whimsical tree festooned with flowers supports garments on hangers. Elaborately carved wooden posts support huge beams. I yearn to move in and spend the rest of my life here. I'm sure I would be happy every day.

Dishes, books, jewelry can intoxicate a shopper who likes to buy local, and we also don't ever stop raving about the food. Even well sated, we can't pass up vanilla rose ice cream with pistachio and saffron: how could you be under the same roof as a creation with so many lyric ingredients and not partake?

Frequently hype creates unrealistic expectations and ends in disappointment. Here the opposite is true. We came, we saw, we get it, and we're beguiled for good having done so.

"Hey, do you know this one?"
—Lisa, when we hear Emmylou Harris, Tricia Yearwood,
Linda Ronstadt, Red Molly, The Eagles, Jackson Brown,
Leonard Cohen, or the Indigo Girls.
—Julie, if it's Billy Joel, the Dixie Chicks, Orleans,
Reba McEntire, or Brooks & Dunn.

TUBAC

Charming

After the highway's march and moan, these streets breathe
the spell of a boy's sigh after that first feminine charm.

Spice wafts, beckons, treating flavor's edge to tickle—
not bite—the tongue, with trained old-school charm.

Presidio history stockades cause and effect along a timeline,
a cord no longer uniformly pinned by its defensive charm.

Sunlit brightness bounces about the chapel, cherished
as one of the showpieces on this town's bracelet of charms.

Silk, bead, and bloom drape time-washed stones as life recedes,
tides leaving tokens of love, death, wrought like a charm.

Color piles, sweeps, sways across clay, imagination canvassing
windows, corners, stoops, shelves, these art works like a charm.

Feet pass, pause, enter, depart, stand, rest, repeat,
impromptu moves welcomed in a town turning on the charm.

"A conspiracy of circumstances."
—Lisa's concise explanation for why things do not always turn out as planned, despite our best efforts.

TUBAC

Santa Cruz County can be seen as the cradle of Arizona's history. Our state's first newspaper began in Tubac. Father Kino, the Padre on Horseback, established Tumacácori a few miles south. The Wisdom family has had a café with a giant chicken outside for decades. (All right, that one's more contemporary.) But Tubac and Tumacácori and the realm between are definitely where Anglo and Mexican culture meld, mix, merge.

I'd told Julie about the unique burial ground there. If the wrought iron writing curved above the entrance is to be believed, this may be the only cementery in existence. Right there, a cemetery and a *cementario* hybridize to produce a place where all can feel welcome.

Unlike many such places for burial and memorial, this is a vibrant, active acreage. You see visits that have been paid in the freshly bright

St. Ann's Parish.

Polished pews glow in afternoon light.

bouquets of artificial blooms, the many mementos and candles that have been left to honor the dead. Even though it's nowhere near Día de los Muertos, there's a sense of celebrating those who have gone ahead more than mourning them. But this time I walk farther. Even here, there are plenty of forgotten souls in deep weeds beyond. Do they mind, from wherever they are? Do they resent their celebrated neighbors? I decide that's an earthly projection: if anything I believe about Heaven is true, these are more like placentas buried after they're no longer needed for life, and for those still here celebrating Beyond.

After walking among earlier residents, we walk among current ones. A whimsical mix of asphalt and dirt streets invite strolling. Charmingly rustic, deeply Sonoran with bright painted exteriors and regional crafts for sale, old town Tubac exudes cheer and welcome. A caveat: nothing is easy to find. Every time we are given directions, it turns out they don't make sense. On the fourth misguided trip in search of a restroom, I'm wondering if this is something the locals do to test the mettle of tourists (although it's probably more about being eager rather than accurate). At the old presidio, a four-walled park, signs indicate the entrance is in the next wall . . . which it is not on our first three tries. Once inside, we're freshly confused about where to find the excavation display.

There's an Alice in Wonderland absurdity to touring here.

Schoolchildren in pioneer costumes are conducting some sort of reenactment under the watchful eyes of similarly attired adults. Seeing the first printing press brought into the state feels educational. Walking past the Pennington building, enticingly for sale, creates an urge to be the next owner of this ancient adobe formed by hand so long ago. I am reminded of a dear friend who amuses her husband by announcing, "I want to live here!" everywhere they go. Tubac evokes this response in me. The pace feels slower; more relaxed fun is being had than in major metropolitan areas, or at least it seems so.

St. Ann's church has been deeply significant to me ever since a man I loved kissed me in the aisle on an empty afternoon. The silhouette of the roofline is as iconic as the Alamo to those who know it. If it isn't beeswax that makes the pews glow like gold, I like assuming it is. Several old women who could have been sent by a casting agent are praying their beads on kneelers, expressions placid regardless of possible tumult in their hearts.

After finding a side door and back door to restaurants that are puzzlingly open but either empty or not serving, patio dining at Wisdom's Café North proves lovely and satisfying. And a consignment shop sends me over the shopping moon. We leave the charms of the gracious white country club for another day, wishing we'd both had weddings there. It continues what we've felt: a place for joy that is calm and quiet, not chaotic and frenzied. How appealing it is.

"If I want anything at all to be OK in my life,
I have to remember that taking care of myself is job 1."
—Lisa: daughter, sister, wife, mother, confidante, road trip buddy, friend,
hostess, board member, ghost writer, employee, most roles
calling her before 10 a.m. every day.

TUMACÁCORI

House of Prayer

Whether one is constructing anew
or restoring:
layers of history are only as helpful
as they are supportive
of new foundations.

Beginnings could be crushed
in the violence that inevitably precedes
any big undertaking—
the ripping, digging, demolition
of objects—clearing—
to scaffold a structure,
then build for bearing
the heaviness to come.

Every tomorrow will test:
is this a true shelter
to stand, face the perils of life,
repel rages, buffer sorrows,
be a place for those who built
and keep it
to rest in the shade of their prayers?

"Just because someone else broke his arm
doesn't mean your broken finger doesn't hurt."
—Lisa, quoting Dana Cooper about why you don't need
to minimize your pain.

TUMACÁCORI

Unlike its cousin to the north, the famous San Xavier del Bac Mission known as the White Dove of the Desert, Tumacácori attracts few visitors, leaving more space and time for feeling nearer to history. I maintain that on some level, remote areas keep more of the past alive: fewer people's thoughts fill the air, or it's less breathed than in crowded places. Tumacácori may be Father Eusebio Kino's first mission in Arizona, but it is far less famous than the calendar icon of San Xavier.

Still, quiet has its charms. When no one strolls past on the paths in the olive groves, it's easier to picture workers among the trees, ancestors of Tohono O'odham whom the Spanish missionaries called Sobaipuri. Between the visitor center of the national historic park and the church

Interior restoration work at Tumacácori Mission.

The mission.

building, only blowing grass creates any sound. It's perfect for imagining the space four hundred years earlier. Tumacácori continued to evolve from when it was first established as Mission San Cayetano de Tumacácori on the east side of the Santa Cruz.

Julie's been deeply immersed in mission research and we both love the candle-smoke tradition of places where pilgrims have come to pray for a very long time. Being one degree of separation from whatever priest or laborer etched the fresco next to the dome fascinates and humbles me. Knowing how many frantic or grateful petitions have been offered in this space imbues it with sacred air. I hope there are field trips from Heaven, because I want to come back here during the 1600s to watch a baptism.

But now the aisle of the chapel is empty. We can walk into the sacristy at the back, thinking of priests putting on vestments to come out and celebrate sacraments with worshippers. The walls are more than a foot thick, making the interior cool. Most of the surfaces show plaster worn off the adobe brick, but there's an elaborate row of crenellated wood in the choir loft. Cautionary ropes as barricades protect from further erosion the adobe mounds that were altars along the side walls.

The building we're in was constructed in the 1750s, though its distinctive dome wasn't added to the chapel until the 1800s. It probably began leaking almost immediately, but the delicately stenciled or traced flowers, though faded, remain present around the edge. Scallop shells were an homage to Saint James, patron saint of Spain, while painted domes and draperies probably framed statues of unknown figures. Faded hues of peacock, peach, and gray remain.

Some years ago, at a Colorado Plateau convention, Lar and I attended a speech on the challenges of restoring and caring for Tumacácori over the centuries. Early restorers used lime, cement, plaster—whatever the recommended material of their time. More recently, they've analyzed and replicated original compounds, which included rabbit glue and nopal paste, and used them again to stabilize without altering what remains.

Written history of such a site tends to focus on the mission's managers, Jesuits, but we are also aware that one man's success comes at another's cost. In the burial ground behind the mission, graves of the Natives, which far outnumber those of padres, are unmarked. That makes the holiness harder to find. But the 593 anonymous souls asleep here surely don't care. Each of us has a season in the sun, and rather than try to untangle what made sense centuries ago, it seems wise to enjoy our own.

"After a trauma, it takes at least six weeks to rebuild the world."*

—Lisa to Julie, after the passing of beloved dog friends Ranger, then Lucy a year later.

—Julie to Lisa, after Mayer nearly died of a seizure.

—Julie to Lisa, after her brother's, then father's, passing within a month of one another.

—Lisa to Julie, when Augie passed the following spring.

—Julie to Lisa, when her mother passed later that same year.

* Note: We do not equate mentally rebuilding the world with feeling settled, or whole, inside it.

ARIZONA INN

A Poem of Hospitality

Even to a first-timer, the inn clearly
stands out while inviting in—
pink poesy in a creamy adobe paragraph,
the frosting flower on a tea cake—
sweeter for anticipating
being treated to a slice of history.

Structured without being formal,
there is character in its lines,
ease in its spaces,
a gracious brevity of design
avoiding clutter while providing comfort
to those taking only a glance,
same as those who pause,
savoring a heightened sense.

This is verse, not banter,
song, not plain speech,
not just talk
made musical by piano percussion.
This is a sweet note of timeless grace
best shared
with appreciative company.

"If your feet are in the fire and your head's ice,
that doesn't make your body temperature neutral."
—Lisa, quoting wise friend Dana Cooper, when Julie sold her first book
the same month that Lucy died.

ARIZONA INN

From knowing the Arizona Inn is the color of sunset on a woman's skin, to the fact that that same woman had it built to give dignified work to men hurt in World War I, there is so much to love about this jewel in Tucson's history, heart, and hospitality trade.

Arizona's first congresswoman, Isabella Greenway King, supposedly brought New York City traffic to a halt because of her beauty. In office from 1933 to 1937, she was as remarkable for her principles and strength, from seating a newly hired Black employee next to her at lunch at her inn to roller-skating through the halls of Congress to optimize her efficiency. It was King who is said to have pulled up her sleeve at dusk and told workers to paint the inn that color.

Her great-grandson Will Conroy is now at the helm of the Arizona Inn (though when I first wrote about it, his charming and elegant mother Patty Doar was manager), and while some things have changed since it opened in 1930, many have not. Pieces of the original furniture crafted by veterans are still in use; afternoon tea is still served in the grand but intimate library; croquet can be played on the lawn as the shadows lengthen over it.

Julie and I meet there in the cocktail lounge, where I've always thought Hemingway should have lifted a glass with Tucson resident and naturalist Joseph Wood Krutch. (Oddly, the man who first showed me this lounge has the same memory, but in his, I am showing it to him. Maybe the place makes us generous.)

This is not even my first meeting with Julie here, and in the back left corner is the seating area where Larry and I were delighted regulars during my Green Valley News and KGUN years: June the cheery server had our rosé and Heineken almost ready when we seated ourselves. The piano player would play "Snowfall" and smile at us, and Lar would remind me the lyrics have only nineteen words. So it was a perfect place to

Balcony at Arizona Inn.

introduce Julie to Larry several years ago. Blessedly but not surprisingly, they both saw in the other one what I do. In fact, when Lar died and I was going through things on his desk, there was a sheet with his six-point printing compiled when he read Julie's book *Barbed,* with page numbers and particularly powerful lines that he was compelled to save for her. They grasped one another's character and value swiftly and immutably, adding another layer of beloved memories in this place.

It's December, and perhaps that's the best time to pay a visit. One fact I learned years ago and hope is forever true: halfway during the holiday season, the soaring tree in the corner of the library is taken down to be replaced with a new one, so guests who come weeks into the festivities still get that spicy holiday-redolent pine scent as they gather near the crackling fire.

Each room at the Arizona Inn is unique; some people establish a consistent residence request, while others want to sample this one with the private patio, that one with the living room (which at Christmas included toys for child guests to play with). Everywhere you look is replete with scenic charm: blue chairs matching the lodge's trim, curving paths lined with blooms year-round, quaint balconies and stairways, old vines shading the terrace by the pool.

Lisa and dad, Larry, at the Arizona Inn, where he would later meet Julie.

There are no bad meals, but breakfast is my absolute favorite, and maybe that's because when my father took me there for the first time, it was for breakfast on Christmas Eve. A new moon of honeydew had a crafted toothpick anchoring one grape and a berry to it; I was besotted and have remained so ever since.

Many of us have added our own private histories to the lovely public one. Tea with a governor, a family toast after a beloved aunt's funeral, a silver wedding anniversary patio ceremony are part of mine. I brought numerous dates here, sketching my metaphor of people sharing shoreline on cocktail napkins. Later, Tom and I listened to palm fronds rattle above us on our private patio, after I reveled in working on a book at the in-room desk. Dear friends married here, and years later I loved getting their first baby the tiniest robe with "Arizona Inn" embroidered on it. (The gift shop is a treasure trove; multiple caps and mugs and pieces of jewelry have come out with me.) Right after you walk in through the main doors usually opened by two quick and gracious staff members, you can look up to the right and notice the long black-and-white photo of the inn during its infancy. Tucson almost doesn't exist around it, meaning you can examine it for a while to orient yourself and see what it looked like. If you do that, know Larry did too—pretty much every single visit. That's just one memory.

If you add your layers of experience, know you join Eleanor Roosevelt in doing so; Isabella was one of her bridesmaids and often hosted her lifelong friend at the inn. A venerable majordomo once let slip that Mrs. Roosevelt "always looked as if she were in need of a good brush-up." I'm not even sure what that is but I'm charmed by it, as by all things to do with the Arizona Inn. It's that kind of place.

"Whatever gets you through the ride."

—Lisa, quoting her brother-in-law to her nephew, who was curled into a fetal position to endure a Disneyland sky ride. Equally applicable to any of life's ups and downs.

Sculpted Apostles at the Last Supper.

GARDEN OF GETHSEMANE

The Gardener's Tale

(with apologies to Chaucer)

One need only pay respect to see
Tucson's Garden of Gethsemane.

We enter as the restorer
tells tales of prior pilgrims poor,

giving naught, but stealing digits
from the famous scene religious:

Jesus among apostles
sculpted as in the Gospels.

The beleaguered craftsman sighs
at how vandalism tries

his patience and his skill—
what they take, he must backfill—

"I had to cut four heads off once,"
when night damage left nobs.

Little's left of the originals,
those first hands, noses, toes,

now they're litter in the riverbed,
replacement sculpture in their stead

both humor and a horror,
constant work for this restorer.

I doubt there is a relic trade,
or that profit can be made

off any stolen phalanges,
yet condemnation's not for me—

mine is not to judge a thief
who'd break off then take a piece

of sacred scene and devout work—
the perp might not be a jerk—

just hungry not to pocket-pick
at fortune's body politic.

Perhaps too often no one heeded,
gave no help or hand when needed.

When hands lift less to put things right,
why shake heads that lack brings blight?

"God's not done with us yet."
—Lisa, quoting Larry Schnebly, then Julie quoting Lisa, many, many times, when we or others were not the best version of ourselves.

GARDEN OF GETHSEMANE

When I first saw the Garden of Gethsemane at the age of nine, I felt like I'd stumbled into an outdoor cathedral full of Renaissance sculptures. When I saw it again in my thirties, it seemed so cheesy I was embarrassed by my childhood memory.

I was curious to see what I would think this time.

The oddest part is the location: it's tucked in a hip pocket of Interstate 10, virtually under the Congress/Broadway exit. There's no reason to expect anything there but discarded soft drink cups and the odd tumbleweed. Instead, here is Felix Lucero's promise to God fulfilled: life-size statues of Jesus Christ and some He loved.

Julie loved its story of origin as I did. As Lucero lay dying on a World War I battlefield, he promised God that if he survived, he would create religious statues in thanksgiving.

Well, after getting distracted from his mission for about twenty years, Lucero arrived in Tucson and was "living rough" around that intersection, meaning unhoused and dependent on the kindness of strangers. Then he bloomed where he was planted: using found objects, riverbed sand, and plaster to create *The Last Supper*, *The Holy Family*, and several other works.

True to the spirit of his gift, the Garden of Gethsemane is open dawn to dusk, free to all comers. Thanks to a cooperative agreement between the City of Tucson and the Pima County Parks and Recreation department, there's adult supervision of the site, and it's locked at night to discourage vandalism.

Under the proviso that it's better to be lucky than smart, while we were wandering about taking photographs and notes, we saw a man, who turned out to be named Greg Schoon, working on a marble arch. He was in occasional conversation with Art, who works in the area and drops by from time to time. Art's family goes back generations here, and he's discovered artifacts on his meanderings. Greg is arguably the best thing that's ever happened to the garden, repairing the sculptures and statues so skillfully

Artist Greg Schoon talks with local descendant Art.

we would not have known, except that I recalled missing fingers and noses that were now replaced.

Greg's impressed with Lucero's skill at creating the plaster people; he says he doubts he could have done such good work with rudimentary supplies. While he makes his contributions to the art with respect, he does not at all have Lucero on a metaphorical pedestal.

"He was no saint; he drank, he had kids with many women, lived under the bridge because he didn't want to go home. A woman came while I was working once, with photos, claiming to be one of his illegitimate daughters."

But Lucero's work, while humble, also speaks to any self-perceived lack of worthiness that might be holding us back from making our own contributions to the world. He didn't have a degree, or pedigree, or even permission: he just put his heart into his art. There are always naysayers ready to tell us why something is a bad idea, or that we shouldn't be going about it in a certain way. Fortunately, Lucero was able to tune that out and create.

The Garden of Gethsemane, with its filtered light and birdsong under utility poles, is a good place to feel awareness of the sacred without being bothered by reminders of the pedestrian. Holiness is not reserved for old cathedrals or even sanctified ground. I think that spirit grows wherever pilgrims seek it.

"We all make sense to ourselves."

—Lisa, quoting a writing client summarizing what he'd learned over decades as a practicing psychologist. We've used it as explanation, consolation, accusation, and observation.

Castaways*

Feel for, forgive,
those thrown
by the triangle—

the father-in-law,
cuckolded, betrayed,
by his greedy son-in-law—

the mother-in-law, overripe
to relish feeling savored, seen
as seductive, craveable,

despite her craven heart,
closed toward
husband and daughter—

the son-in-law, standing stud
for a woman who needed nothing,
wanted everything—

the daughter, abandoned, slipping
into cold death, no passion's heat
to warm drowning memories,

the cornered, keening for mercy
after being played by some angle,
against better judgment.

Confess now: who among us
hasn't cast,
or been cast, away?

---

* *Tiradito*: one thrown away, from the Spanish verb *tirar*, to throw away.

EL TIRADITO

The Sinner's Shrine.

"There's a lot of ground between marrying someone and never seeing them again."
—Larry Schnebly, pointing out our tendency for either/or thinking.

EL TIRADITO

It goes by several names, and shreds of many stories cling to this rustic adobe shrine on South Main in Tucson.

El Tiradito translates to "The Little Castaway." It's also known as the Wishing Shrine and the Sinner's Shrine, with accompanying legends of tragedy like wisps of stories caught in the wrought iron and candles at the site.

What's for sure true is that it is on the National Register of Historic Places and the only shrine in the nation dedicated to a man considered too evil to be buried in consecrated ground.

He was actually buried nearby—the southwest corner of Meyer and Simpson, according to some. Shifts in landownership moved the site since Juan Oliveras was laid to dubious rest after being murdered by his lover's husband . . . who was also his father-in-law. The framework of the legend is that in the 1870s, Juan, a young ranch hand, became besotted with his mother-in-law. Under "there's truth and then there's facts," he may or may not have been caught in that woman's bed by her husband before being axed or stabbed.

Decades have passed since my last visit. When I was a Pima County Victim Witness volunteer in the early '80s, my volunteer partner Jerry Harwood brought me to see it during the wee hours, after most businesses are closed and streets are deserted. Being on duty until 3 a.m. led us to all sorts of places during times of stillness. Perhaps because he found my peripatetic love life rich in drama, he figured I'd appreciate El Tiradito.

I did, even though some of the prose of the legend gets pretty purple: series of further grisly deaths with torture and suicide woven through them. I skip those, and prefer to focus on understanding how passion can blur judgment even in people who regard ourselves (yep, taking ownership) as fundamentally good.

Julie loves all things with Sonoran influences in Arizona, so she's visited before. It's much more established than I remember, and far better attended; the relics, candles, slips of paper, and photographs are tenfold more than anything I saw back in the day. Back then a rickety wrought iron candle holder for rows of votives was about all the structure there was, compared to the current walls with an Alamo-like curved top. It reminds me of returning to a beloved dive bar and seeing it now shiny clean and selling t-shirts.

This is a place where the sacred and profane don't just meet but come crashing together: skulls and saints, grinning ghouls and beatific babies, fading photocopies of loved ones' photographs and scores of wax from extinguished relics lit for prayers bear testament to a panoply of types of grief and remembrance.

We see tiny rolled petitions stuffed in crevices in the adobe like eels in a coral reef, although it's also evocative of the Western Wall. We wonder about stories behind some of the items: how many are for sinners, how many for saints, and how often do those categories overlap, at least in human opinion? Trust Tucson to preserve and celebrate the wry truth that we are not to judge anyone, let alone those who have gone before us. Why wouldn't Juan Oliveras deserve this physical outgrowth of his worst decision?

I'm wary of embracing some of the tendrils that follow his murder. Maybe "every story deserves a top hat and a stick," but I like the simplicity of pausing to pay tribute to the weakness and impetuosity of youth (and come to think of it, older versions of us as well—the woman was no spring chicken), and to consequences suffered. If someone didn't make just a few glorious mistakes, they probably missed some amazing experiences to tell around their own campfires later in life. El Tiradito seems to celebrate that spirit. Here's to it.

"Fatigue makes cowards of us all."

—Larry Schnebly, quoting Vince Lombardi.

—Lisa to Julie and vice versa once a week, and twice or thrice that during the COVID-19 pandemic.

Doors in the Yuma Territorial Prison.

HEADING SOUTHWEST

The iconic peak seen from I-10.

PICACHO PEAK

Halfway Points

Who are we to discount, casually
demote something
standing wholly for itself
as “halfway there,”
so eager to claim progress
we confuse *halving* with *having*,
as though journeys, points,
never get the half,
or better, of us?

"From way out here, all of this is just interesting."
—Lisa, interrupting Julie's breakup lament before Lisa also says, "because I know, know, know, this is not where the story ends for you."

PICACHO PEAK

Picacho Peak is many things to various audiences: the site of Arizona's only true Civil War battle; a mecca for the wildflower equivalent of leaf-peepers; a stark landmark along Interstate 10 to many motorists who love to complain about how boring that drive is, the way recruits love to complain about military meals.

It is two additional things to me.

The first one is this: Picacho Peak is what makes Newman Peak the Most Ignored Mountain in Arizona.

I was introduced to Newman Peak while flying over it in a small plane. The pilot pointed out that while it's considerably larger than Picacho, everyone is so arrested by Picacho's distinctive shape across the road that virtually no one notices Newman.

Mary on her way to the tomb on Easter morning, on Picacho's south flank.

Since then, I've done my part making it up to the poor rough, ungainly sibling across the road from Picacho. Admittedly somewhat nondescript, Newman is 4,500 feet—although I found three different heights online. And Picacho's about 1,500 (I found four different heights). It deserves at least a nod. But who among us hasn't at some point felt like Newman Peak, as the world celebrates someone else in our airspace?

Picacho even gets a state park, mentioned as having been on the Butterfield Stage route and open to hikers.

The second thing Picacho is to me comes from my father, who used to make the Tucson-to-Phoenix drive weekly, absorbing details of the landscape. He pointed out what he called "Mary walking to the tomb on Easter morning," and I saw it instantly, following his finger. When you approach from the south, it emerges at a certain point on the first third of Picacho at the crest: her small figure in a hooded robe walking toward the cave farther south. I've nodded to her on every trip since.

Two picnics from my youth involved the wildflowers. I was less than moved by the blossoms. (Neither romantic relationship lasted; maybe that soured me.) There's also the ostrich farm, which enthusiasts extol; the variety of species to see there does sound impressive. And ostriches were a cash crop in Arizona for a time when their feathers adorned women's hats in lavish profusion.

Picacho is also where a dear friend hiked himself out of his comfort zone and had to suffer the ignominy of being rescued by professionals. He would be the first to tell you: don't do that; you can be charged.

In addition, Picacho Peak is one of our beloved linguistic redundancies, being the English and Spanish words for "Peak Peak." (Table Mesa and Rillito River do the same thing.)

All this leads me to posit that Picacho may be one of Arizona's treasures that separates novices from seasoned appreciators of our state. Most residents would instantly resonate to the distinctive crooked-hat silhouette, whether it be replicated in a sketch or as a chocolate in a custom box. Many of us have photographed it in various moods: swathed in fog, stark against a blazing sunset, or decked out in springtime color.

As for the Civil War battle, for years men fought to be included in the reenactments, since the battle involved only 13 Union and 10 Confederate troops (the Union reported 3 wounded, 3 killed, and Confederate losses may have been 3, with 2 wounded, but that number is uncertain). The battle occurred as the California Column of about 2,000 Union volunteer troops moved toward Tucson, where the 120 Confederates who had claimed the town as Southern would surrender the presidio without a shot being fired once the odds were made clear.

Should you drive by, or decide to stop, before you leave the area, please give a nod to the east side of the road, where Newman Peak (in my head, at least) yearns for a scrap of the attention Picacho gets. Thank you.

"There's a pony in here somewhere."
—Larry Schnebly, giving the punchline to an old joke about
the optimist reveling in a room piled with horse dung.
We quoted this many, many times during the COVID-19 pandemic, funeral preparations, health procedures, breakups, and other unpleasant events that occurred during the writing of this book.

YUMA

Stop Where You Are

How much we miss
just passing through,
dismissing locations
because departure
is more celebrated than arrival.

A steamboat could paddle by,
catfish surface to sun,
cottonwood froth billows
to stray along a silty trail, but
these "not there yet"
middle distances
may as well be prisons, places
we only want to be far from,
never mind
that by missing them,
we miss so much of the journey
to where we want to be,
we might not even know it
once we get there.

"The most dangerous six words are 'we've always done it this way.'"
—Larry Schnebly, gently advising that a new approach may not be so bad.

YUMA

Talk about a place that gets no respect.

If 20 percent of Arizona residents go to California in any given summer, many of us beach commuters see Yuma. We may even stop in Yuma. But it ends there. We aren't there to appreciate it for itself: we're in it for the restroom, the gas, the food, or all of the above.

On family vacations until adulthood, we had to stop in Yuma and eat at Denny's. This pushed arrival time back by excruciating minutes, and I hated it. (Which is why now my trips to California begin before dawn and I get to eat lunch there, having arrived by then. The brother I visit likes to amuse us both by texting about seven, "Are you almost here?")

Then, on those bygone days, on our way back home, the car crammed fuller with mouse ear caps and sometimes portable beach chairs and big

Julie's photo of the banks of the Colorado River in Yuma.

hats, we would stop again. On the return trip, after marine-layer mornings and highs often in the seventies, stepping out of the car back across the border in Arizona blasts you with air so superheated you can't believe you didn't notice it a week ago. And, adding insult to injury, for most of us it's still a long drive home.

Yuma stands between us and our vacation. Yuma matters only because it's where you cross the Colorado River into the next state. All this explains why Yuma didn't rank high on a list of places I would go on purpose.

But now I have.

The time to go was in January. You can see we're already setting ourselves up to succeed. The temperature is moderate. This way it doesn't feel like punishment to see the river, and the Yuma Territorial Prison.

It's interesting to see the river from any vantage point that isn't on the freeway out of a car window, and we walk down to the water's edge, where there are eddies and sandbars and breezes. It's pretty—all water is pretty, pretty much—and welcoming, an accommodating host to water birds and wildlife alike. I look at it and picture this same water coursing through the Grand Canyon not so long before now, where it fought for a place. Here it streams serenely past, with plenty of whatever water regards as elbow room.

Up above on a bluff is the Territorial Prison. I've read about it—how infamous bandit Pearl Hart set up a media tent when she was here, and apparently the guards fell under her thrall the same way reporters from big-city papers did. We know she had a child while she was serving her time; there must have been some privacy. (Or a gangbuster of a story no one ever wrote.)

Exhibits contain objects of common use when the prison was housing mostly men in a distinctly inhospitable environment: pen knife, leg irons, and locks. Photos of former residents share the space. The cells themselves interest me more.

The rock walls, some built by inmates, are massive, heavy, and thick with locally quarried boulders.

Do places hold feelings? Does air breathed long enough in desperation and fear contain palpable molecules of those emotions?

We can't know for sure, but just as there seemed to be faith in the centuries of prayers and candles inside Notre Dame, the prison feels grim and desolate. Beyond the fact that it is deserted and away from most of society, there's a scrim of hopelessness to me.

View from inside a cell, Yuma Territorial Prison.

It's never fun to contemplate not being free, especially in a place so barren and hot that even those of us who can speed away in air-conditioned cars don't necessarily want to be here. How much harder to have the worst time of your life unspool in this often-oppressive climate.

On the plus side of Yuma, it's always nice to see the completely theoretical and yet real demarcation line that means we are either home, or in a neighboring state. Yuma's got crops. Yuma's got full-time residents. And yet, well, it's still mostly a way station to me.

"Hit the ball, drag Fred."

—Larry Schnebly, giving the punchline to the following joke:
A guy goes golfing, and his partner has a heart attack on the first hole.
Arriving home hours late, he explains to his wife that Fred had died.
"It must have been terrible!" she says.
He says, "It was. Every hole it was hit the ball, drag Fred."
We use it to laugh at our self-assigned and misguided overdoing.

A sight in Parker.

HEADING WEST

LAKE HAVASU

Fantasy Lands

Many of us never wonder
at how water transforms our lives.

We live as though entitled,
usage by Divine Right,
kingly volumes drawn
for leisurely showers, car washes,
fountains, water features
prominent in mythologies.
With it we lord
as Ladies of the Lake,
captains of our own vessels,
developers
of our own destinies.

Watered, even improperly, dreams grow.

Like a lake from a river
bridged by an icon:
what's above and below
from far-away lands, fantasies
made real
in a state saturated
with expectations for more,
as though these flows
don't need us to wake,
roll over to reason,
for what magic can there be
in water left untapped?

"Do you have decaf coffee?"
—Lisa, at lunch.
—Julie, after dinner.

LAKE HAVASU

Lake Havasu illustrates perfectly that it takes only three things to sustain life: land, water, and sunlight; and that water is the element that can be moved.

There used to be too much land and sunlight here, but adding water changed everything.

Driving up the road alongside the Colorado River meant I could no longer claim that water makes any landscape beautiful. It doesn't do a lot for the view from AZ 95 en route to Lake Havasu City (and other points). So many people have staked out their wee slice of paradise-by-the-sea that the ticky-tacky dwellings are kind of all you see driving in. But I'm a visitor on their turf, so my disdain doesn't matter. Add construction cones

Across the human-made channel on the Colorado River.

narrowing us to one lane for miles with no workers present, along with a chain of oversize RVs crawling to (their) paradise, and I'm not feeling the love. As if that weren't enough, I'd looked forward to seeing Coffee Ern's in Parker, and don't. Blast change anyway.

However, once I arrive and meet Julie and the dogs, I'm reenergized, remembering why Lake Havasu City is worth a visit every so often. Julie recalls learning of a Holy Roman emperor who was not holy, Roman, or an emperor. Likewise, this is not a lake, we are nowhere near Havasu, and it's more burg than city. But here are the good parts:

1. It's over-the-top tourist, clumsily but earnestly mixing two themes. The first is twee British culture in honor of the London Bridge that was dragged from the Thames after 130 years of loyal service and reconstructed in this desert, where blowing sand scrubbed away the coal smoke that previously made it black. From the only replica of the gold stagecoach British royalty still uses on occasion in the London Bridge Resort lobby (and gazing at it I see why there's only one) to the Ice Cream Shope (neither *shop* nor *shoppe*) near the fountain with spitting lions just down from the red phone booth, it's for people who may never see the real thing but can dip a toe in faux London. The other culture is a slapdash Margaritaville: sand, boat rentals, and ice cream versions of tropical cocktails on patios, where good-natured people unabashedly savor the vacation culture, however lowbrow it might appear to some. Okay, to me.
2. The London Bridge really is wonderful, with the visible bullet holes from World War II dogfights, and tunnels running inside I yearn to see. It is a classic one degree of separation from thousands of peasants who trod it almost two hundred years ago, plodding through a world so removed from this that it's fun to try to picture what they would think of the new digs.
3. That a whole commercial metropolis has grown up around this unlikely pairing of blank desert and world treasure proves Arizona has space for dreams. Robert McCulloch, known for chainsaws from his McCulloch Motors, made a fortune and wanted to purchase the Leaning Tower of Pisa and was Pised he was turned down, but his second choice turned out to be far better. There would have been no reason to dredge a channel and invite the Colorado River to flow past the tower, as it does

Julie, Lucy, and Augie taking a break.

under the bridge. While Lake Havasu is not lovely from every vantage point, walking by the water (especially in February instead of summer's 110 degrees), watching Julie's doggies Augie and Lucy mobilize gulls as we appear, and getting to see a sailboat silhouette as well as some Han Solo–worthy old scows, makes Arizona's West Coast pleasant . . . worlds more pleasant than it would have been if Arizona hadn't provided the sunlight and land to give McCulloch a place to plunk down his dream.

4. It's been almost twenty years since I had that piece of coconut cream pie at Shugrue's so heavenly I've never forgotten it. Not only is the restaurant still open and still serving the pie, but Arlo the server has come to Arizona from Connecticut to live his dream. By the time we leave, he's unspooled his story to us and surrounding tables, leaving business cards in his wake. Robert McCulloch would be proud.

Postscript: we walked at dawn. Watching the water under the lightening sky made a perfect farewell gift from this place. Nature is always at its best without throngs of people. I better understood why residents love living here. And as if that weren't enough, driving back through Parker I saw that Coffee Ern's is still there after all: it's just that the sign on the incoming side was broken. Seeing it on the outbound trip was like encountering an old friend. Now I'd go back much sooner than I thought I would as I was driving in.

"The best sign of a good trip is not wanting it to be over."
—Both of us. Every time.

Giraffe at Papago Park.

CENTRAL

Sunlight shows the clarity of Fossil Creek water.

FOSSIL CREEK

Ode to Fossil Creek

Scraggle-scratch, flora as stubble,
cragged rock faces seeing double:
each turn twinned with yet one more—
a dirt road apt for hardship lore—

hazard-scape, both wide and deep,
and yet some unseen water creeps,
homing trees along its wend,
lone streak of green as we descend.

Gravel bends and bumpy grit—
more miles than we have chat to chit—
then, glory! parking! stiff foray
to creekside views of liquid play—

flow so pristine I'm tracking fish—
this water desert's dearest wish.

"Which way to the water?"
—Lisa, to a picnicking family we found camping on the flat between parking lot and audible creek. It really was that hidden. Or we were that impatient. Maybe both.

FOSSIL CREEK

"Damn, not damn."

This piece was first conceived as touring a dam, another dam, and a not dam: Granite Reef Dam, Roosevelt Dam, and Fossil Creek.

The reason the last is a "not dam" is that Arizona Public Service decommissioned the dam site at Fossil Creek in 2005, restoring twenty thousand gallons of water each minute down travertine falls. This was a major gift to Arizona, doubling our number of official Wild and Scenic Rivers from just the Verde to the Verde and Fossil Creek. Nature lovers and conservationists rejoiced; in a world where nature seems imperiled, something was getting better rather than worse.

Julie and I had planned to visit the three sites for one piece, but life intervened in terms of pets and health and parents, making the plans not match up with our deadline. We decided of the three, Fossil Creek ranked highest on our list.

Larry had extolled the wonders of the place after a visit, describing with enthusiasm the incredible clarity, the multiple waterfalls, the lush foliage on both banks. Figuring "what's not to like?" we set out, with minimal planning except putting "Fossil Creek" into the map app.

If adventure is when you don't know what will happen, this qualifies. The sixteen-mile road is one of the three roughest I've ever done, sharing that dubious honor with the roads to Grand Falls and Chaco Canyon. We ruefully pass a wrecked car, picking our way across the gravel fan that shows where the driver had lost control and spun out.

Finally we arrive at the first parking lot, where a sign showed us the length of hikes involved in seeing various waterfalls. We are . . . daunted. Fall has not come in with October; any hike would be hot. We decide to shoot for the closest waterfall and call it.

What Lar had not told us was that Fossil Creek rivals the Grand Canyon for hiding in plain sight. Every time I approach the South Rim through light scrub and scrappy trees, I marvel that all of a sudden,

Water rushing over rocks in Fossil Creek.

you are beholding this unexpected cathedral of space and sculpture, this wonder of the world. Similarly, at Fossil Creek you walk a dusty path in unrelenting sun until there's a bit of green. Incongruously you hear the water and continue with more confidence. And there it is. Rushing, tumbling, racing, roaring over falls, both singles and doubles. Greenery abounds, from soaring sycamores to fragile reeds. As we accompany it downstream, a wider pool lets the water slow to an almost imperceptible drifting.

Never have I seen such clear water in nature. I'd have supposed that any watercourse in Arizona would have some silt or mud. But this is like being in a huge fish tank, it's so clear; traceries of tree shadows, fish are visible. This is a very different creature than its river and creek relatives in other parts of the state.

A family of two parents and a son are swimming, laughing and cold. We greet one another and move on. Having to leave the bank, we bushwhack through some weedy growth to get back to creekside farther down. The music of water is infinitely calming, and appreciably cooler than feet away in the sun.

After Julie sets down her hat and picks it up to see ticks, we have to do an assiduous check. Ruefully we relearn, remind ourselves, that nature is all of a piece: the stunning, the troublesome, majesty and midge-sharing space. Reluctant but driven by hunger, we agree we've experienced Fossil Creek and trudge back to the vehicle in the heat. Reversing the road trip, we pass an incoming tow truck, presumably for the wrecked car.

This drive to find food points out a significant difference between this and most other excursions we've made. Fort Bowie was the only other place that lacked any services. At the South Rim there are many distractions; even West Fork has food nearby. Other than rudimentary rest stop facilities, Fossil Creek is splendidly isolated. Its rustic status will keep it less trash-strewn, less traveled, so in the big picture it's a good thing. But part of me thinks a charming café just before the first parking lot would really enhance the experience.

Driving slowly is a nuisance but extra talk time; we analyze gender differences, weigh the worth of relationships on a trouble-reward ratio, and solve problems of a few people who haven't asked us to do so.

All this makes me reflect on road trips in relationships, the way tide-pools indicate the health of the ocean. How much and how comfortable the conversation, how symbiotic the need for rest stops, how much laughter, how much understanding are variables that measure the quality of the company.

And again, Julie's a ten.

"Here are the rules: don't judge, don't compare,
release the need to understand, trust the process."
—Lisa, quoting her sister.

So far, we're better at remembering the rules than following them.

STATE CAPITOL

Desert Island

This museum ponders like
a roadrunner hunched in tortoise shell—
time is kept, flightless,
a place to float remembrance
in a backwater of commerce—
rusty warehouses, machine shops
mirror more than neighbor,
work gone—ever unseen—
little new except what gets lost
in the local traffic patterns:
one way, keep out, restricted.

There is no welcome here.
Not even a sign.

For the dogged dodging barricades,
there is little representative
of the mainstream channels
where most in this state
make their living.

All the greater challenge to those charged today
with ensuring a future worth remembering.

May they never be
like the clutter of relics landed here
to sit, not serve,
while oceans of need rise
around them.

"It's just one more one more thing."
—Julie, describing COVID-19 time.

STATE CAPITOL

Our state capitol is like Smithsonian Museums, free to all comers. It's a hybrid of impressive exhibits and Arizona's attic, where both wise and eccentric curators have left their marks.

The capitol is located at the west end of our capitol mall, between Washington and Jefferson Streets, another repository for monuments both powerful and puzzling. Here the viewer may swing from being deeply moved to oddly puzzled. First, patterned on the Capitol Mall in Washington DC, ours is named for Wesley Bolin. Why? Because he was our shortest-serving governor, only in office five months? Or because he was our longest-serving secretary of state before that, at twenty-eight years? Wouldn't it make more sense to name it for George W. P. Hunt, our first, third, fifth, and seventh governor, who served a total of seven terms? (In a way, the more you learn about Arizona government, the more sense it makes that the mall and capitol should be . . . quirky.)

Among more than thirty monuments is one for K-9 officers felled on duty: a bronze dog that's noble and sobering. There's also a 9/11 memorial, which came under blistering criticism for the collection of phrases mounted overhead. Changes were made that make some of the inscriptions impossible to read unless direct sun comes through the die-cut letters at exactly the right angle. It's nice to honor Arizona pioneer women, but a statue from "Daughters of Utah Pioneers" seems odd. That's near a bronze for Civilian Conservation Corps workers, which is again a fine thing, but one might wonder why of all the noble causes in state history, this earned coveted real estate. Military veterans of every war since statehood and all fallen first responders are honored. The firefighter monument is the only one on which every name has a small Arizona flag carefully placed by someone, and it's poignantly sunlit the day we visit. Those of a certain age may be moved by the Vietnam War memorial, the only one where the statue shows true desperation and fatigue rather than frozen nobility or cliché resoluteness.

Guns to Salute the Fallen includes the names of all Arizona World War II veterans killed in action (cleverly, room is available if more are discovered

Winged Victory weathervane on copper capitol dome.

over time) between guns that bookend the war: one from the USS *Arizona,* since its bombing at Pearl Harbor got us into it, and the other from the USS *Missouri,* where the final treaty was signed. (There's a fun story about this. Then–secretary of state Ken Bennett very much wanted to obtain a USS *Arizona* gun. The Department of Defense was reluctant; only two remained. But the department countered with an offer for a nice USS *Missouri* gun—seven of those were available, and, at sixty-six feet, storage might be a challenge. Proving why he is a strategically successful politician, Bennett offered to take one of those off their hands . . . if they added one from our namesake ship. He got both.) Also here on the mall is a USS *Arizona* anchor, where children have played for decades. Their voices and laughter lighten an admittedly somber setting.

We walk down the mall to the capitol building. On the impressive copper dome is the seventeen-foot *Winged Victory* weathervane, who swings at her moorings in the breeze against the Arizona sky. (Some say she's survived so long by being able to turn with the winds, a valuable political trait.) Behind her looms the executive tower, offices for Arizona officials added when the original capitol was outgrown—which began even before the building had been completely moved into. The worst of midcentury architecture shows in the House and Senate buildings. These are on either side of the Wesley Bolin Memorial Plaza stretching east from the capitol, which at least does make a place for demonstrators, photo opportunities, and a truly impressive piece of petrified wood.

Constructed of native stone, the capitol is older than the state; it was built to prove we were grown-up enough to graduate from being a territory. Does it say something about us that the winner of the Design Arizona's Capitol contest used plans that had been rejected for Missouri's capitol? It's a nice illustration of Arizona as a place for second chances if nothing else.

Inside, grade school classes, lobbyists, and tourists stop on the ground floor to peer up into the elaborate dome through a hole created by mezzanines on each floor, and down at the mosaic state seal. To the left the USS *Arizona* gets another display, beginning with a map of Pearl Harbor, showing that eight ships besides our namesake sank in the attack. Past that is a section of the *Arizona*'s hull. This packs a punch, putting the viewer one degree of separation from the carnage and tragedy of that famous "day that will live in infamy." The ship's elaborate silver service was being cleaned instead of stored in the officers' mess on the ship, and so saved from sinking, it's now displayed in glass cases here.

Another glass cube holds the empty champagne bottle that President Gerald Ford commissioned for the final two remaining Pearl Harbor survivors to toast their fallen comrades. Apparently none wanting to be a solitary drinker after the other three passed, the remaining four of those met in 2013 to share the champagne, which was surely much more enjoyable than drinking it alone. After that event, a placard tells us, the National Park Service lowered one of the two original glasses over the sunken ship, where survivors' remains could be interred until all the veterans had passed.

Less historic but more cheerful is the Gratitude Train exhibit. A lot of us may not know before we visit the Capitol Museum (most of the old building has exhibits scattered through rooms and hallways, although State Library and Archives headquarter here in a high wing) that in 1949 the United States sent 80 railroad cars full of badly needed food and supplies to France, which reciprocated after the worst was over by collecting 52,000 gifts from citizens and businesses to fill 49 cars, one for every state at the time. Besides the embroidered handkerchief, paintings, and toys, a sign says 1,990 others of those gifts are in the museum's collection. Because this is twenty-first-century public space, a coffee shop and gift

K-9 statue in Wesley Bolin Memorial Plaza.

shop occupy the other first floor wing during our visit—sometimes things change here.

Strolling around elicits a lot of "who knew?" in most of us. Soaring paintings by Lon Megargee, known to many for Lon's at the Hermosa Inn, the restaurant in his old adobe home-turned-resort, fill one hall. If they were prose, they would be purple indeed, but they are nice 1913 tributes to the state. *Spirit of Arizona* seems downright whimsical, while *Water* clearly embodies the sensual, slightly reminiscent of a painting that would hang over the bar in a saloon. I remember on our sixth-grade field trip the boys did not want to move along from the sprite in her very diaphanous robes.

As with any eclectic buffet, variety rules. As a longtime fan and devotee of the Rough Riders with their life-thirsty leader Buckey O'Neill, for me seeing the flag they carried in Cuba (made in one night by seamstresses back home) elicited reverential chills. I am looking at the very fabric that fluttered and drooped under hot sun the day their gallant leader died . . . as well as the day my shirttail great-great-uncle Billy Wallace sustained the wound that resulted in a metal plate being put in his skull. This bold play by some field surgeon resulted in Flagstaff winters giving him burning headaches, which meant he was living by Oak Creek when my great-grandparents moved there. But back to Buckey; his widow Pauline also intrigues me mightily, and that increased when I read that after his death she married his brother Brady. Who later killed himself.

"Lagniappe" is an unexpected bit of extra, a piece of candy with a grocery order, for instance, in New Orleans. The lagniappe of this visit was coming across a telegram, with the romantic heading "Night Letter," giving the Arizona delegation waiting breathlessly for word of statehood news that the current judicial provisions were preventing us from joining the Union. I was already focusing my camera when I saw the signature: Eugene Brady O'Neill. He's the brother Pauline married after Buckey died. I almost swoon with historical curiosity and love of surprises.

Proving that even if we take the same trip, our journey is distinctly our own, Julie loathes every aspect of the sights that beguile me so—as is probably evident by her poetic contribution. I bask in a friendship that has so much room for difference.

"For new order to appear there must be disorder."

—Lisa, quoting Belinda Rosser's lesson in a management seminar, during the COVID-19-induced shutdown in summer of 2020. Then Christmas 2020. Then most of 2021. Then with each variant afterward. We lost count.

PAPAGO PARK

siting the local waterfowl.

Water in the Desert

A new season officially begins:
spring—eagerly awaited—
the pandemic winter
an uninvited guest
long overstaying the patience
extended by coerced hosts—

we emerge from isolation's cold
stumbling toward normalcy—
warmth—
only to be stopped,
queuing for vaccines
as desert travelers might
at a badly mapped well:
hurried, harried, hyper-focused,
humorous in our delirium
that it be our turn,
our time—finally—
a different time,
punctuated by exclamations,
rather than the yearlong ellipses
we've all been living.

Our cars dot the makeshift lanes
of Phoenix Municipal Stadium
like the golf greens driving
through the nearby desert,
one welcome turn at a time,
starting then stopping,
not a flow
but a stumbling stutter step
of one finding her feet.

To be turned loose
a second shot later—vaccinated—
is a dash toward freedom,
embracing life,
but first, each other,
out of our cars into morning
fresh with creosote shade,
a wash of relief to be together,
an oasis
as marvelous and everyday
as cattails in the Papago ponds,
friendship—like water in the desert—
too easily taken for granted,
too precious to be without.

"I like two kinds of coffee: I like it free, and I like it hot."
—Julie, adapting a beer toast from college.

PAPAGO PARK

Any day in nature is a day well spent, but the one when Julie and I met at Papago Park occupies an honored setting in the museum of memory. On a shelf by itself, it was our first venture back out into the world after more than a year of quarantine: the day we both got our second COVID vaccines.

Technically, we would not be fully immunized for another two weeks—appropriately, Easter Day. But since we were outside the entire time we felt safe meeting one another, walking together with Augie, reveling in a return to a wider world than the one fenced in by fear. It felt like great gulps of freedom and clean air.

This area is home turf to Julie; I'd been only several times before, when attending events at the Desert Botanical Garden or shepherding our

Julie enjoying our first vaccinated day back out in the world.

children through the zoo decades ago. I'd never walked along the always-surprising sight of water in the desert, next to the canal.

Nature's artists—water, wind, and time—did some fine work here: whorls and crags, scoops and scallops, are sculpted in the red rock. We admire an egret's flamboyant takeoffs and landings; we search the shelves of sandstone for bighorn sheep. Mostly we relish being able to move about, occasionally passing other strolling savorers of being outdoors.

We talk about Arizona Governor George W. P. Hunt and his fascination with all things Egyptian, which led to construction of his pyramid mausoleum, visible up on its lofty sandstone spot. A robust man with a preference for white suits, he inspired later governor Raúl Castro by pointing at him as a barefoot boy on a whistle stop in Douglas, saying in Arizona anyone might grow up to be governor. Hunt also made an impression on Flagstaff doyenne Viola Babbitt, who later recalled that as a schoolgirl she attended a luncheon where the walrus-mustached figure displayed appalling table manners. Everyone has facets that lie beyond the first line of their biography, we agree.

We spend some time wondering why it's still called Papago Park: if the name, a Piman pejorative, was offensive to the Tohono O'odham Nation, shouldn't it be changed? Do they live far enough away for indignation to be ignored? A later web search would turn out to be fruitless, but we hope and agree it's surely a matter of time before more respect is shown.

Julie wants me to see the rock house within the zoo's boundaries and gets us tickets. She's familiar with most of the animal residents, who are taking the sun at this time. I'd not known about our Arizona flamingos, who are more white than pink because of the coloring of their diet (in other words, not shrimp).

The rock house is charming. Arizona's "old" buildings would be laughably new on the East Coast, but we live here in a place where adobe crumbles quickly and people weren't building with anything else until fairly recently in terms of recorded time, so we delight in this quaint construction with details of an earlier era than the twenty-first century's more common brick and stucco. Ruby's House was built in 1935 as a residence for the caretaker of the fishery that eventually became the Phoenix Zoo, and we discover that weddings there are popular and frequent. Well, that's good.

Eventually, lack of food and water make strolling feel more like forced marching. We debate how to rejuvenate without putting ourselves inside with a crowd probably composed of at least some people who did not receive their second liberating vaccination this morning, or even a first. We try to enter one restaurant, but Julie discovers she just can't. Finally, a line for a coffee stand gives us the chance to get snacks while remaining completely outdoors, and we find an alfresco table where watching the world go by feels familiar and free. Disneyland, Sea World, parks, zoos, and gardens haven't been options for some time. It feels a little weird, like when I was a child, wearing shorts and a sleeveless top for the first time in the spring: newly fledged, a little vulnerable, and very free.

When we part back in the parking lot, we are starting to feel the effects of a second shot earlier in the day, but we agree the fatigue is a small price to pay for getting to saunter among our fellow Valley residents, shored up, safer, ready to return to more communal living after a very long year.

Lisa: "How long has it been since we last got together?"
Julie: "Um . . . was it Havasu?"
Lisa: "Oh, surely not *that* long."
Julie: "If we can't remember, then it's been *way* too long."

LON'S HERMOSA INN

View from the patio of Lon's at the Hermosa.

Best Picture

"Let's meet at Lon's," Lisa suggests,
first-name-basis tone fond,
familiar.

"Where?" I ask.

I was a debutante
but grew up on a farm,
making anything north of the Salt River
unreal to this Gilbert girl.
Paradise Valley sounds starlet,
red-carpet plush,
flanked by Phoenix, meaning business,
and Scottsdale—eye roll—
bucking tourists.
It's "PV" to its friends,
for whom Glendale is Lincoln,
Forty-Fourth is Tatum.
Paradise must be the place
where streets change.

"The Hermosa Inn," Lisa explains.

"I don't know it," I confess, thinking
I'm from the valley of the Valley—
south of the Salt,
well beneath social radar,
nowhere that news happens.

Lisa knows news.
Lisa *was* the news.

"Oh, it's wonderful," she assures me,
"I can't believe you haven't been there!"

Understand:
Lisa is as capable of condescension
as I am at mapping Mars.
Neither of us have ever been there.

"There's a lot of Phoenix I don't know,"
I mumble, feeling mouse level,
the scuttle and twitch
of the commute
to my central city, all-girls high school
scratching at me.

How insecurities can trap us.

"It's right around Thirty-Second and Camelback,"
she says, "north of the canal, east of Thirty-Second."

Well, now I'm home.
Any farm girl can find her way
around a canal.

I find Lon's really is a home,
ranch-style, hiding its size,
as old grand homes do.

We are here for headshots.

Lisa offered to take them
much as a big sister might
hold my clammy hand
going to the doctor's office.
Shots of any kind and I
have never been friends.

"You remember Lon's paintings
at the capitol?" Lisa asks,

striding across the courtyard
seeking photo-worthy light.

In my eyes, she is expert:
at history, photography, writing,
femininity, dating, love, curiosity,
learning,
an encyclopedia that reads
like a greeting card.

I remember
studying the murals upstairs
at the capitol—
(why does Lisa know everything
at altitude?!)—
"Irrigation" had held me,
a goddess standing astride
a full channel flowing between folds,
pouring into a planted furrow,
alfalfa a spring green
extending behind her toward orchards
at the foot of mountains—
an Arizona of dreams—

one doesn't depict a loved place with labor,
no, here was a naiad, gorgeous—seductive—

of course Lisa knew her, and her maker.
Lisa, legend in my mind, wasn't in that picture
only because she was busy—as she is now—
making pictures for others,
who, getting to look at her,
simply must smile.

"There's a time to make money, and a time not to lose money."
—Julie, quoting Brian Jackson, whose financial advice is applicable to other churning times when adjusted expectations, patience, or both, are the best approach.

LON'S HERMOSA INN

Lon Megargee did what so many do: came to Arizona and knew himself to be home. Adopting a cowboy artist persona, he talked his way into a contract to paint murals for the new state capitol building, even while we were still a territory—he was that charismatic.

What began as the adobe studio and house Megargee built when he arrived in the '30s is now Lon's at the Hermosa, a restaurant bearing his name, and Lon's Last Drop, a bar named for his sketch of a cowboy emptying his canteen into his hat for his horse. The rest of the Hermosa Inn came later but is so true to form that most of us don't know what's original and what's additional.

Walk into the courtyard entrance and feel transported back in Lon's time of construction, flush with mural money. Brick walkways, niches, and sconces among abundant manicured gardens and lawns welcome you, with background music of relaxed conversation and the splash of the central fountain.

First invited here by Arizona political doyenne Carolyn Warner (we both showed up in black with major turquoise jewelry), I've been bringing new recruits ever since. It's somewhat like showing someone the Grand Canyon; I almost envy their first look. But each visit layers another memory on the place for me.

Megargee loved women (he married seven, although that number may be approximate), art, and celebrating life. An oft-repeated anecdote came from his fellow Arizona artist Ed Mell, he of the sweeping scapes of virga and canyon. At a reception, Mell modestly opined that Megargee must have dashed off smaller works to support his lavish lifestyle, affording Mell the opportunity to acquire three of them.

"I was at a similar reception in San Francisco," Mell said, "and mentioned I had three Lon Megargees. A woman in another group immediately attached herself to me, laughing at my remarks and touching my sleeve frequently. I was impressed someone there knew Megargee's work. After a bit she said, 'Did I hear you say you have three Lamborghinis?' and when I clarified myself, she remembered she had somewhere else to be."

After our initial visit for headshots because of the plethora of picturesque southwestern settings, we have made it our valley version of the Arizona Inn: the place for celebrations, even if they're just because it's Wednesday. The chubby birds hopping about the patio tables, the sweep of tree branches dropping foliage bits that the staff accepts as inevitable, only add to the awareness of being immersed in Arizona outdoors at its best. (Although breakfast by the beehive fireplace in the grand old dining room is intimate and perfect in its own way.)

To stay at the Hermosa Inn reinforces the feeling of being a valued friend of the artist, tucked in his lavish guest quarters (which are pitch-perfect in style and period while offering every modern luxury). Massive beds with crisp linens and a view of the fire on the hearth; private bricked courtyards along tucked-away paths leave one wondering how long it would take the staff to discover you'd not left after checkout time.

Whether it's bringing southern cousins for a cocktail, sitting outside with visitors who decide they want to live here, or a guest who likes dive bars finding out he's loving the alfresco short rib breakfast hash, every meal here is an event.

The library is a traditional meeting place that feels like the scion just stepped out for a smoke on the patio; there are lovely old comfortable sofas in the lounge. But the ultimate, at which Julie and I wondered what catalyst would be deemed worthy of the expense, would be a feast for us and ten fortunate people in the private dining room that's housed in the wine cellar. Down the narrow stairs into the cool stone walls, it invites an event you'd never forget, and would remember fondly and often. Even if we find ourselves living that dream, there are still 364 remaining nights that year open for others' banquets.

"Once you've gone down with a ship, any little tremor on your next voyage is going to make you run for the lifeboats."

—Lisa, explaining a disproportionally large reaction to a comparatively small event.

—Julie, either quoting Lisa or substituting with a(nother) dear friend's version: "If it's hysterical, it's historical."

Lisa taking a photo of Megargee's *Last Drop* in the lounge.

A calved-out section of rock in Oak Creek's West Fork.

HEADING NORTHWEST

The elk surveys his world.

PRESCOTT

Here to Stay

We want to be at Courthouse Square—
regardless of whether we've been—
wishing to arrive fully somewhere,
a stand-out, not a stand-in.

The square is a place we go to be met,
even if it's just for the day,
by smiles, impressions, exchanges, events,
or a treasure we find on the way.

Fulfilled wanderlust, satisfied feeling—
being here, without need for a "there"—
each and all sides, corners, angles appealing
to remain as some part of the square.

Courthouse Square finds us what we sought
as we lap, again, around the block.

"When your world gets smaller, your emotions seem bigger."
—Julie, quoting a wise summer camp director.

PRESCOTT

No matter where we go, each of us visits a different place. The experiences we have serve as workers building memories unique to us—even if we're with someone who was there with us before.

When Julie and I reach Prescott's Courthouse Square, I'm practically reverent. We've already made a mutually relished coffee stop at the grand dame of hotels, the Hassayampa Inn. Built the year my father was born, the Hassayampa is to me the place where Tom and I fell in love. But there's also room for other memories: my friend Pam teasing me about needing a headquarters on a frozen holiday trip we made with baby Sedona, fascinating lunches with Jerry Emmett, who at 102 told me of her one great love while we celebrated her birthday in the Peacock Room there. And now, cups of the beloved nectar of any morning with my poet friend. I point out the elk atop the Elks Theater across the street, where the spectacular trio Red Molly sang, literal feet from my transfixed self.

I have a confession: even though I have some small reputation as a passionate Arizona historian, I was not always so. At thirty-one, I was with Lar in Flagstaff when he suggested we drive back through Ash Fork "so we can see Prescott's Courthouse Square."

As self-chagrined as someone who might say that they stole from the collection basket as a child, I confess my first thought was, "Well, but that would take longer." It was that year when my understanding of Larry's bromide that "journalism is history on the fly," meaning history is a part of every present, ignited my passion for Arizona's past.

Did it start here? Certainly, there's much to revere. The Buckey O'Neill statue on its huge granite stand, brought in to receive the sculpture of a Rough Rider (which then had Buckey's name bestowed after he died). I tell Julie about how in true Arizona fashion, the statue itself didn't arrive in a timely manner, until finally a railroad agent was dispatched to find it. Find it he did, forlorn on some siding in New Mexico, and he got it here at the true eleventh hour. Buckey's paean of love in the Prescott paper to

Fireplace and intricately decorated ceiling in the Hassayampa lobby.

his wife, Pauline, is both priceless and purple; I think he used twenty-nine rhapsodic adjectives. I remember all this in this plaza.

The Christmas lights that bathe it annually in holiday glory after the faithful gather in the shivery darkness for the first lighting are magical. It was the night before that event that Tom and I held hands and ran to the cornerstone, where he kissed me, changing the course of my life in the best way possible.

I also see photographer Mike Schmidt and me here, when we were the Northern Arizona Bureau for Channel 3. A mother hesitantly approached us with two exquisite little girls: were we part of Arizona's Family? (Such was the power of the campaign David Miller had created.) "Every night, after we say our prayers, we sing your song," the mother said. Mike and I were both touched at what seemed to us a rather odd reaction to what was essentially a jingle. But when it was sung, over video of the sweeping vistas and stunning scenes of our state, I rather shared her reverence. (Part of the lyrics: "We are proud, we are free . . . Arizona's Family.")

Today Julie and I decoupage another layer of vignettes on this place. Hungry after hiking Thumb Butte, we revisit the bar and grill where my dad and I came the day the Centennial year countdown began: February 14, 2011, so a year before our one hundredth birthday. Visiting the same spot with its view of Courthouse Square, I rhapsodically describe Arizona artist Ed Mell's stamp being unveiled and a meeting where I found out Ken Bennett used to make up irreverent lyrics for a song the last night of every legislative session he'd been part of. (A year later, Lar and then Tom would help me sell hundreds of Centennial books at the Best Fest in the same square.) Well-nourished and reenergized, Julie and I saunter the four streets surrounding the square.

Now we're indulging our inner cowgirls: Julie has ridden for decades, and I like cowboy boots for the plucky stalwart Western feeling they give me, and for how surprisingly comfortable they are. We admire, and she tries on then buys a splendid pair that she will actually wear to ride, always able to remember where they came from. We pass the Harley Davidson store where I bought Tom Christmas ornaments, and the ice cream shop where I've always wanted to buy something, anything. (That still hasn't happened, but I get to look forward to it.)

We look at coffee, at earrings, indulging in the timeless practice of both window shopping and examining various tempting offerings. We agree shopping is as much seeing you don't need anything as it is finding the perfect thing. We greet the happy doggies and their people who circumnavigate the same four sides we do, around the majestically pillared seat of justice rising high enough to provide significant shade. She remembers a good time at Hotel St. Michael I didn't experience, but now think of whenever I return.

Looking at the gazebo, I remember when the kiddos were small and my dad and I brought them here after introducing them to Robert Euler, the man who found split twig figures left by early residents of the Grand Canyon. A photo from that day shows Sedona in a sunbonnet and Rye holding the tiny figures we brought from home as a homage. Part of me wants to buy a sunbonnet.

But it's enough to know I can. We part fondly, agreeing that the air in the Courthouse Square has now been autographed by both of us one more time, and we are richer for having done so.

"Maybe we can have it all. Just not all at once."

—Julie, remarking on the blessings particular—possibly exclusive—to each phase of life.

Thumbs-Up

A piñon-tipped smell of sunlight
edges toward our dangling feet,
competing for attention
with coffee waft,
daybreak, and each other,
seated on Thumb Butte for sunrise.

My camp crush—
slick as cool granite with the girls—
sits   strangely quiet
while my heartbeat climbs, yet
trekking switchbacks.

In a movie, sound swells
before a first kiss.

Here silence s u s p e n d s,
as travel lids flip, tap, stutter.

"Want to get bagels?" he asks.

What

sheer

descent,

to manage
a thumbs-up.

THUMB BUTTE

Thumb Butte silhouette.

"I didn't know that was an era."
—Lisa, remembering her newsroom career at KGUN in Tucson, and the general mindset of our twenties, when we think we'll have what we have forever.

THUMB BUTTE

For as many times as I have looked up at Thumb Butte from Prescott, I've never seen Prescott from Thumb Butte. Today that changes. Prescott has drawn me in many guises: to cover the Oldest Continuous Rodeo and parade for KTVK-TV3, for the famed Courthouse Lighting, later for a ceremony in the original state capitol, to kick off Arizona's Centennial celebration. Now I'm coming with Jules to make a different pilgrimage: a hike that was part of her growing up.

We're experiencing classic higher-elevation Arizona weather: warmish in bright sunshine and downright cold in shade. Julie explains that the more scenic of the two trails to the top also takes longer. I choose speed over view, since every vista will be new to me and therefore worthwhile.

It's always interesting to see what someone else loves. This scenery entrances her. The low-mountain, high-meadow combination of conifer and deciduous trees, with accompanying growth of ground cover broken by areas of duff, surrounds us for long stretches, and as we climb, we occasionally catch an opening showing how far we've come. Prescott has gone from being out there to *down* there. But I'm wondering how much memory colors every experience. To me there's almost a lack of beauty in the surroundings she is transfixed seeing. Do I do that with places first experienced with my dad? Or am I just not genetically gifted with the appreciate-juniper-and-duff gene?

Jules relays the first unforgettable hike up this trail. We talk about the huge rock, twenty-eight tons of granite, that was brought from these hills to serve as a mount for the Buckey O'Neill statue in Courthouse Square. That kind of monument works for a man who got his nickname by "bucking the tiger," or playing an old card game called faro, besides also serving as sheriff, mayor, and posse member, as well as journalist and miner, scattering legends from Tombstone to the Grand Canyon before his bright life was snuffed out as one of Teddy Roosevelt's Rough Riders in 1898 Cuba.

The Buckey O'Neill statue on its huge granite boulder.

Jules cruises up easily; I pause and breathe from time to time. She's serene at each stop, getting to gaze about and smile. When we get to the trailhead there's a choice of directions, and we take them both: first the southern leg, out to an overlook, then the northern route. It's like being the goldfish in a bowl looking back at viewers, having been where is now "from the other direction" so many times. This is a vastly expansive vista all the way out to Mingus Mountain, where my grandfather got lost on a hike and was so chagrined the next day that he'd caused the fuss of a search. We also look toward Mayer, Dewey, and Humboldt with the old post office by the highway, the ribbon of road with dozens of stoplights through Prescott Valley. Best of all, I get to see my beloved San Francisco Peaks.

For as many times as I have seen Thumb Butte from Prescott, it's wild to do the reverse—not as extreme as getting to look at the earth from the moon, but in that category.

"It is the mark of an intelligent man to hold contradictory thoughts simultaneously."
—Lisa, quoting F. Scott Fitzgerald when ambivalence seems the best we can muster.

Hearth from Mayhew Lodge at West Fork.

WEST FORK

Back Home

This is a thin place—
veil between real and imagined,
breath before a song,
wonder as a gift opens,
as space does here—leading
into Mother Nature's back room,
quilting in gold and ocher,
river rocks tumbling
in collected admiration.

Water laps like her puppy
joggling, swaying in its course,
eager to play, pawing at newcomers
preoccupied in its midst.

Sycamore tea—tang and spice—
is served all day.

This is a nursery for laughter,
giggles gurgle
from the eager creek
chuckling along the walls,
tickling the leaves.

Our steps sip at its gladness
as we grasp for what to say,
how to give thanks for all we take in,
trees shaking their heads,
declining our attempts,
hushing, ushering us along—
we may muse as we meander—
they'd rather we be fully present
than miss any part of our visit
searching for words.

"Take every hour as a separate job, be kind in it,
and don't let your pride be hurt."
—Lisa, quoting Kathleen Norris's *The American Flaggs*
when priorities feel murky.

WEST FORK

West Fork never disappoints.

The hardest part is one of the nicest parts, which is water crossings. And the most confusing part is also the best part, which is that I never come back out on the exact same trail I took in.

Parking is easier when you come early, as I always prefer. Pretty soon you come to the ruins of Mayhew Lodge. It would be difficult for me not to try to imagine what it looked like before it was a fantasy ruin of garden and walls. But this way is even more picturesque and evocative; it could have been recently abandoned by characters out of novels this way. My dad has told me of a date here, swimming with a daughter of the Fain Ranch

Ranger investigating aspen leaves.

empire, "although we both knew she was way better than I was." No pool remains, but the story tickles Julie as well. On another trip Tom and I had taken advantage of relative privacy, an experience I wrote into my book about great-grandmother Sedona, partly because revered author Diana Gabaldon champions romance belonging not only to the young. Meals, sleeping, showers . . . to me, everything is better outside.

Today it's her and the doggies for company, which is easier for me than the time it was my daughter and her friends, and I kept worrying about someone breaking an ankle on my watch. The doggies are surefooted and easygoing, sometimes having to take a figurative knee when another dog comes toward us. But they're well-behaved, and seeing them savor the scents makes me wonder how many things they can pick up that I can't. I get sweet spicy creekness. But they get all that plus moss, oak, pebble, probably fish. So I have to let my eyes do more of the feasting than my nose.

West Fork has so many kinds of beauty, and all so different from the Oak Creek Canyon we generally admire and photograph. In here are soaring sheets of sandstone, many showing their age by the desert varnish that has been laid down during one patient rain after another until the color is dark and rich, like permanent virga drifting down. In here are massive boulders, which must have made a mighty sound when they landed after hurling and crashing from some place up above I can't see. In here are the fresh light green of ferns, the deep rich red of fallen leaves, the clear yellow of leaves in transition.

Just as you can't step in the same river twice, you can't hike the same West Fork twice: time of day makes light and shadow play alter the scenery, even if you recognize a feature you've seen before. Sometimes the creek water is icy and rushing, other times desultory and fairly warm. (I step in it at least once no matter what, never on purpose, as we navigate various points over slick rocks to make a crossing.)

Even though there are people and animals in the area, most vistas are flora rather than fauna. The canyon is so narrow it feels intimate, contrasting with the open environs around Sedona. Sometimes you hear a canyon wren, that delightful twee-twee-twee-twee in a descending scale that sounds like the bird is tumbling happily downward like a child on a water slide.

I've never gone the entire six miles in, and never known how far from the end I am when I turn around. Today we finish when we are about half an hour past hungry, and almost inhale our hearty Indian Gardens Café & Market lunches. Then it feels good to sit in Julie's truck heading out while the doggies take a well-deserved nap, lulled by the susurrus of the road and rhythm of the rocking up the switchbacks.

West Fork is a place I rarely think of unless I'm there, and I should change that. Bringing up those serene scapes with their vivid hues does me good. It reminds me that even when I don't see them, such lovely places are waiting for another visit.

"The only thing God doesn't have is hands, so ours are needed."
—Lisa, deftly demystifying Incarnation and most of the rest of Christianity.

San Francisco Peaks from Hart Prairie Preserve.

HEADING NORTH CENTRAL

Early builders in Walnut Canyon combined artisanship with existing infrastructure.

WALNUT CANYON

Picture Time

Scuffed toes poke past pavement
for a shot at the cliff dwellings
never fully captured, even now,
that we know of,
curve and shadows
a mantle for mysteries.

We can approach,
but will never be close
to understanding
what we can picture,
just never frame quite right.

I savor the postcard sense
of strolling its rims, this high
desert island ducking wind,
shifting sun to shade, shrugging
that many won't make its rounds,
marvel at life sprung from rock,
promontory of prehistory,
hard for anyone to climb in,
then out of, time to itself
ending as ever, abandoned
to other migrations.

"This is my first response. Others may be better."
—Lisa, quoting a wise counselor.

WALNUT CANYON

Even in Arizona, where adobe doesn't always stand up to the ravages of time, we can visit some homes of those who came before.

Proving that centuries ago was as today, and real estate was about location, location, location, Walnut Canyon stands out for being better protected than most early building sites.

Tucked into walls of Kaibab limestone crevices and under protective shelves just east of Flagstaff, these rock shelters seem downright welcoming. Even more so when you think of the heavy snows that would have fallen just outside the cozy dwellings, where residents could watch with enjoyment instead of in freezing misery. The natural overlooks that shade our trail once provided wonderful porches for the people who called this home for some eight hundred years, leaving around the thirteenth century

Peering into enigmatic rooms in Walnut Canyon.

for reasons unknown. It strikes me that they called Arizona home far longer than later white settlers have—everything we've built goes back about half that time, if you start with the missions of Father Kino. And in our cities, even hundred-year-old buildings are rare and remarkable.

I've never actually seen the stream on the canyon floor, but in the West, pretty much every canyon is carved with water as the main ingredient. We're only ten miles out of downtown Flagstaff, but it could be hundreds of miles—as well as hundreds of years—away. Except for the staircases by the visitors' center, there's little sense of civilization.

We're told it was the women of the community who built the rooms we peer into as we pass, a small fraction of all the ones in the canyon. They used the limestone rocks with a golden clay as mortar, and the curved walls display artistry and a sense of aesthetics. It would take a very different person than I am not to be stirred by all we can never know about those talented people. Did they work in groups like women around a quilting frame, using the time to laugh and visit? Did one act as leader, choosing placement and construction of walls? The results of their talent is all that remains of them.

I swear, by the time we're two-thirds through, I feel like I've gone up and down at least 1,200 feet. I'm never great at altitude, and this takes every bit of my reserves to complete. I haven't had the pleasure of living in Flagstaff for a while, so starting at about seven thousand feet wipes me out.

I was surprised when Julie included this in her list of favorite Arizona places. Having come once with Mike Schmidt when we were the Northern Arizona Bureau had felt like quite enough. Seeing the rooms was interesting, but mostly it felt like a long tough walk (really only a mile?) with not much return on the investment. So it feels good to be willing to try again. I'm curious to find out what I missed the first time that captivates her so.

Truthfully, I find myself thinking, "not a great deal." I'm reminded of a string quartet named Bond that recorded a song called "Explosive." The first dozen times I heard the song, it unspooled in my mind a movie trailer of my life, or sometimes a life I wish I'd lived: people on horseback galloping across moors and massive libraries in ancient castles. I sent it to my brother Lindsay, eager to hear him rhapsodize. Instead, he sent back, "I kept thinking, 'make the noise stop.'" How could generally like-minded people be affected so differently?

This is the canyon equivalent of that song. I was more than ready to get back out long before we actually did. Somehow the mystical magic Julie responds to eluded me completely.

Truly, the best part was knowing we'd earned a lavish lunch from the exertion. I felt bad, as if something in mc was broken. But I didn't think that when it was Lindsay left unmoved, so I shouldn't create a double standard. And I guess it's good to know that even extremely simpatico people who are often breathless at shared discoveries or responses to things sometimes simply aren't aligned in their reactions.

Would I go a third time? Only if the company were as good as Julie. And then, only for that company.

"I make my own lunch!"

—Larry, giving the punchline to the joke about the guy who opens his brown bag at noon to complain to his friends, "Tuna, again. Every day, it's tuna." The friend finally asks, "Why don't you ask your wife to give you something else for lunch?" The man shoots back, "Leave my wife out of this! I make my own lunch!" Oh, yes. We do too.

FLAGSTAFF

Highest Return

Not a hub—not centered with spokes—
nor a crossroads—too many find their own way here—
more like a race arch, a Janus of Journeys—go
explore, yes, discover—remain a bit longer—
visit, learn—we cannot be still
in its peaks and valleys, cones and canyons,
any more than we can still be the same after adolescence.

As pilgrims before its sacred gods we are bumbling—
dust that shouldn't gather on kachina wings—
restless before its profundity, undeserving, yet devout,
zealous to be in its glory again, but we cannot stop:
worship cannot be forever. We have to work,
we have to keep going, so we can return.

"We'll clean it up in post."
—Lisa, using an old newsroom term to forgive Julie who, on deadline and under stress, said something with lots of feeling and too little thought.

FLAGSTAFF

If I were told that the world would be destroyed except for one place that I got to choose, I'd keep Flagstaff.

Besides its jewel-like setting and frontier history, it's the greatest repository of my own memories. To go there is to create yet another layer of lovely images on the already rich archive. I can get almost oversaturated in recalling events now over, but never gone.

At the train tracks where Beaver Street crosses, I can almost watch my mom's folks coming off the train when I was two. I can see my brother Lindsay shooting the Peaks through the spokes of the lumber wheels for the Arizona Centennial book. I can see the live shot we did as Channel 3's Northern Arizona Bureau when seemingly the longest train on record

The Babbitt Building, across from Hotel Monte Vista.

lasted through our entire video package and pulled out of sight just as I finished speaking, leaving photographer Mike Schmidt and me laughing in jubilant gratitude and wonder.

When Julie and I strolled downtown, I pointed out a fire escape on the side of the Orpheum. In the 1950s, when my dad worked at KGPH radio in the Weatherford basement, he and his boss, Gene Phillippe (the P in the call letters) might walk out after signoff to find that fire escape ladder lowered. It signaled that the theater owner had a new film in to show them in a secret post-midnight screening with libations included.

The Weatherford itself is where my dad asked my mom out on a first date; it's also where I saw my first feather-headdressed Native person in the lobby, and distinctly remember at three years old wondering what on earth one says to such an august personage (though I lacked the vocabulary to express it at the time).

The university campus is its own treasure trove: my grandfather earned a master's there and for one term he and my dad roomed together in Taylor Hall. My folks were the first head residents at Peterson, and I can stand again where we took a photo in our Arizona State College shirts when I was two. Then, as a student, I worked at the Blome Building, where Mom had done practice teaching—after the ten-year-old version of my dad had attended the same teaching school.

As half of the Northern Arizona Bureau, I could walk to work from my Cape Cod condo just below the hospital down to the Monte Vista. Our office was up the short flight of stairs off the lobby. I showed Julie the front desk, where back in 1989 a clerk told me a young man had dropped off a t-shirt from the San Francisco earthquake. My consternation at missing him prompted said clerk to ask if I had a crush on him. I denied it so vehemently I realized it was true. And later Tom Heidinger parked the massive satellite truck outside on Aspen to take me to dinner. . . . Later still he parked it at the hospital lot to hike through the snow to my condo. He proposed with a ring purchased at the Flagstaff Mall. Our first snow walk was in Buffalo Park, where decades later I walked alone in the rain keening, after dropping Rye at NAU. (That's a big bone-deep bandage pulled off, even with the second child.)

Back downtown: what's now the plaza was a concrete wasteland when the powwow was held there in 1991 and one of the dancers invited me to join him; his wife quickly gave me the required shawl. Later, Tom and I

The Peaks behind the lumber wheels at the train depot, Flagstaff.

and the kids had lunch there. Flagstaff welcomes layers. Almost across the street is the sandstone building with "Masonic Temple" still visible above the main door; Larry recalled a few years ago that his parents drove in from Parks for meetings inside, leaving him in the car to babysit sisters Patsy and Paula. "In the winter, they'd come out every so often to turn on the car and run the heater." What sounded like child abuse to me was a simple memory to him, devoid of discomfort or judgment. And across to the north, Julie and I look at the lovely old sandstone courts building, where I covered the Ricky Bible trial in 1989 and later got a jailhouse interview. Memories light the corners of my mind, indeed.

Beaver Street Brewery was Food Town when I was a baby, and before that the first store to sell actual ice cream, right there from a case, without a special soda fountain shop. Later a bunch of us feasted there after a Grand Canyon raft trip, then after a run on Schnebly Hill Road celebrating my dad's seventy-fifth, and much later my nephew's rehearsal dinner.

But more of the small moments loom largest. My mother went to Our Lady of Guadalupe as a college student to weep for a fiancé overseas. I didn't know that when I visited as a lonely seventeen-year-old not ready to be away from home. And Nativity on Beaver, that splendid stone structure soaked in prayers and the scent of beeswax, once creaked and moaned like a ship in a gale when I was praying there. Later I photographed our daughter in that space performing in the Jazz Madrigal Festival.

The best part is that there's no cutoff. You can keep creating experiences in perpetuity. Now the Monte Vista is the coffee and wine bar where Dad and I would take gelato, looking out at the Mission Ice Cream sign on what had been McGaugh's bookstore with its scents of tobacco and popcorn. What was the Pure Food Bakery, where the whole town took a coffee break in the '40s, became the Downtown Diner with a standout trout and swiss cheese omelet. It's closed, but I bet it's between acts: one of us will be there again.

Some changes are more welcome than others: I yearn for the days when train whistles blew all day and night; now it's a rarity. But these too may come around again. For now, the caw of ravens and rustle of wind in the trees on Aspen that turn yellow as a harbinger of autumn is all the music a soundtrack in Flagstaff needs.

"If you bring out what is within you, it will save you;
if you don't bring out what is within you, it will destroy you."
—Lisa, quoting the Gnostic Gospels. The best explanation we've found for why we write.

Virga over the Grand Canyon from the South Rim.

SOUTH RIM

Remake

My life is a new production
since the last time I was here.

As scenes open I am set
on a loop, the road I traveled
one way, threading, losing momentum
with every forced turn.

Now the set reruns:
junipers scraggle along paved paths,
squirrels scurry, kids spill,
parents push, hikers spike their sticks
into mule-trodden ground.

There are millennia in every second,
the canyon a strata of stories.
While my friend's play here
as on a silver screen,
mine feel overexposed,
and I am reeling.

"I don't know anyone who has changed as much in as little time as you."
—Lisa, commenting on Julie's metamorphosis from married rancher to single (published!) author and poet over the course of their friendship.

SOUTH RIM

Memories of visits to the South Rim of the Grand Canyon are as layered as the rocks we gaze at there. And each trip adds a new one.

While my recollections don't reach back billions of years, it's startling to realize that the first time I saw this place, I was seventeen. (While Arizonans take pride in having one of only seven World Wonders, we tend to be sanguine about seeing it—it's not going anywhere.) Joe Rosenbaum's mother and I took a bus trip from Flagstaff, and having been told that hiking back out took twice as long as hiking down, we pushed ourselves so hard on the ascent that we had more than an hour to sit in El Tovar's gem of a cocktail lounge. That's a touchstone: I've been on the patio with my father, Larry—seeing him with a beer and that view is seeing someone in their element. Another time it was a late dinner with a photographer I knew who was shooting a documentary with Dale Shewalter about the Arizona Trail. This time it's a warm lunch on a chilly day with Julie and Lucy, well-behaved on her special blanket by our feet, aware of every movement of a standard poodle a few tables over.

Everywhere we walk is lined with visions of trips past. Running along the trail toward the Sunrise Service site in 1991 with Lar, I tripped and didn't sprawl, but miraculously recovered. I can also see an earlier self, sitting on a bench as people have throughout time, staring at the panoply of jewels across black velvet that is the star-strewn night sky over the gorge. My sister-in-law, Nancy, took her first look at the panorama and burst into tears of awe. Over there is where I saw now-husband Tom park KTVK-TV's behemoth satellite truck between the Hopi House and the sidewalk, like putting a yacht into a one-car garage and making it look easy.

Now Julie and I walk Lucy far out toward Hermits Rest, where I bought my first baseball cap and gasped seeing the actual Colorado River again—I'd only seen it from raft trips before that. We marvel at the gradual gain in altitude, seeing the village we seemingly just left a dramatic distance below.

The photographer comes around from behind the camera to celebrate.

We visit the wonderful fireplace in Bright Angel Lodge, where architect Mary Colter used the rocks from each layer from the Colorado River to the rim. We marvel (as I do each time) at the intrepid Kolb brothers' building their quaint abode seemingly over thin air. Before leaving El Tovar, I get to visit the farthest stall in the basement bathroom, favored because it has a wide windowsill where I used to put my earpiece and briefcase as a television reporter, then my diaper backpack as mother of small children. Today it's just phone, camera, and jacket.

All of this omits the actual reason we come: to see the Grand Canyon. At eighteen, my reaction was that yup, it looked like all the gas station calendars. I couldn't wrap my head around the spires and cliffs and vistas dropping away like draperies. But after rafting, it made marvelous sense, and each visit is a reverent pilgrimage to the place and all we can't see from up here looking down.

I wrote for that Arizona Trail documentary, "Some of nature's finest work is on display here, created by her artists: water, wind, and time." The canyon is both unchanging and varied; each degree of sun's shift changes the view slightly. Sunset, of course, is the dazzler: hues of copper, cinnamon, taupe, and rust deepen until the watcher sits in sepia-toned reverence. I also wrote, "There's no encore after this greatest show in earth. But another performance always comes at sunrise."

There are more places to see than a day allows. We won't visit where storyteller and pioneer John Hance is buried, with other leading citizens. We won't spend time in the second-floor El Tovar lounge where ladies took tea, or stay in Buckey O'Neill's cabin on the Bright Angel property. But we have laid down yet another layer of experiences to remember on future trips.

While it's shocking to me that Julie hates this almost as much as I love it, her memories being of a far different stripe, I hope that this one visit may ameliorate her aversion to what is to me deep and sacred ground.

"A moment of peace is worth every war behind us."
—Lisa, quoting the Indigo Girls' "You and Me of the 10,000 Wars"
when Julie has "sudden" success finding just the right plot, poetic form,
phrase, diagnosis, medication, plumbing solution, boyfriend, coach,
or other moving target.

CHAPEL OF THE HOLY DOVE

Defaced

—names scratching chair backs,
pews, tabletops, rafters,
doors, windowsills, book covers,
door stops, dispensers

pencils left for sad,
        sad signatures
self-sabotaging,
as stated on surfaces
requiring regular cleaning

need for sanding or disinfectant
seems the antithesis of any memorial—
like a shrine in a bathroom—

here, a house of cards for prayer
I am too uneasy to face—

"That's got to go in a poem."
—Lisa to Julie, who's muttering about shrines in a bathroom on the way to the car.

CHAPEL OF THE HOLY DOVE

Many of us have passed this tiny place for decades on U.S. 180 driving to and from the South Rim of the Grand Canyon: a tiny A-frame building. Its roof rises, widening on the far side to provide through the window a better look at the San Francisco Peaks, the Great Sentries of the North. The building sits unoccupied all by its lonesome on the side of the road. This time I'm with Julie, and that makes all the difference. "Let's stop!" she says. We are the only ones there at the time, though others enter before we leave.

The view of the Peaks is grand, though I now realize I've never seen a view of them that was any less grand. With walls of local pine above carefully fitted volcanic rock, this place is clearly a labor of love. There's no one making money off our visit, no one getting to hear compliments. It's open as a sheer gift to people the builder would never meet. That's rare and special.

Inside you can read about this Chapel of the Holy Dove. It tells about a sole physician serving the Grand Canyon, Watson Lacey, coming here with his wife on days off to gaze at the Peaks for respite. "They wanted to give travelers the opportunity to share it," the plaque says. It's on a corner of ranchland he bought in the '60s, and after his brother and nephew drowned, he sought solace in God. Building this to honor the Holy Spirit eased him somewhat. The land is in his widow's trust, and after a vagrant's fire burned it, volunteers rebuilt it.

All lovely. However. Some travelers decided to claim it as their own by writing their names on the wood. Others piled on. To the point that now if you look up at the rafters, you will probably not think of any higher power—you will instead see graffiti left by people who thought they were deserving of being seen. Or, putting the kindest face possible on it, wanted to forever link their presence to this place.

We had a river guide on a Grand Canyon trip who walked on rocks instead of on sand when leading hikes, so people behind him would feel

Many simply drive past the little building on U.S. 180.

they walked in fewer footsteps, and were perhaps some of the few to experience this. In a world where "take only pictures, leave only footprints" preserves the experience for future visitors, these scrawled names in a chapel are startling. I suppose because people see someone else already wrote here, if Johnny jumped off a cliff, they would as well.

Does that matter? Is it worth getting my feathers ruffled? I don't know. But while I walked in grateful, now I'm walking out cranky. What is it in people that wants to make it all about them? And what is it about me that cares to judge them?

Neither of those is a good look. Not a good fit. Maybe it's a little test, to see how we react and in so doing teach us something about ourselves.

Backlit from the inside, the chapel's beauty shows without the graffiti.

Regardless, Lacey deserves thanks for giving us all a place in which to ponder while gazing at the Peaks. Your impressions may vary.

Now if you look up Chapel of the Holy Dove online, you read that many people have married here. To do so, they paid no fee, made no reservation. They simply came. All that's asked in return is that they clean up after themselves and don't deface the property. That's pretty uplifting, although the request to not deface it seems to have been ignored by hundreds of others. Still, a free place to solemnize a union? The Laceys did a good thing that's still blessing lives.

"Some people are easier to love from farther away."

—Lisa, summing up the need for re-setting relational boundaries.

Wide view of one of Wupatki's enigmatic creations.

WUPATKI

Casting Back

Past Time considers himself
a collector, an enthusiast
delighting in recording details
from rich and spare accounts.
It's not the stories he prizes
but their tellings,
much like a jeweler
might admire a stone
for its facets: the more angles,
the more reflections.

"Great love heals greatly."
—Lisa, sharing one of the many reasons she celebrates her marriage to Tom.

WUPATKI

Of all ancient structures left us by early tribes, to me Wupatki stands out the most.

Beholding the spread of a three-story building behind the visitors' center, looking west, you're in the enviable position of not being able to tell what century it is. Go to the Alamo and there's a rent-a-car business or a dollar store nearby; walk to Notre Dame and the way people are dressed gives you context.

But standing where Wupatki's residents ground their corn and skinned their game, the time could be right after they left the area. The hush is the same. The view is the same. The difference is that you drove here.

Hopi ancestors settled here around AD 500, leaving us today about one hundred rooms to peer into at the main pueblo. The best time to visit is just before the visitor center closes; you have the area mostly to yourself, and the light makes an even bluer sky contrast with the red elaborately fitted rock construction. I tend to visualize a runner out on the plain, bringing shells, copper bells, or parrot feathers. For all its splendid isolation, this was on a major trade route.

Arizona has plenty of sites abandoned around 1200, but few are so intact. Without getting embroiled in the impossible quandary about how much stabilization and restoration should take place, I bask in the original rock work that shows a builder's awareness: several rows of round rock above most of a sandstone wall. Then, as now, people cared about decoration and design. "We are not so different," those stone rows say to me.

Two features here welcome flights of fancy. One is the ball court, which evokes tribes far to the south playing ball games. The other is not a human relic but a geologic gift: a blowhole. Air pressure dictates whether a strong constant wind pours up out of underground cave systems or rushes downward past.

As I sit there, taking in the breath of underground (and wondering fleetingly what spores might come), I first picture early residents linking

Where human construction meets geological formation.

the change in direction of airflow to perhaps an awakened deity. Then I feel foolish; it's far more likely the observer thought, "The air pressure has changed."

Whenever I come, I try to get a sense of those who lived at this matchless place. We're told most daily activities took place outdoors. If I align myself right, can I be exactly where a young woman brushed her hair, aware of admiration from someone she hoped to impress? Where did a mother nurse the latest baby, watching the older ones play? Where did a young man, setting out on his first hunt, look back up to see the community watching? Then, why does it matter?

I suppose because it is human to yearn for connection. Wupatki was left with few clues or messages for us. Perhaps I feel a bit bereft, abandoned like the elaborate layers of sandstone by the benefactors. Or simple curiosity prevails: what links this site to a more Aztec culture than most of what remains in what we now call Arizona?

Puebloans who settled here were a hospitable bunch; found items show they traded with what we know as Sinagua, Navajo, and other peoples. Still today, Zuni, Hopi, and Navajo people honor these grounds.

Julie and I don't have theories. We wander. We observe. We talk only a little. It's a place of long-ago presence, although not in a forbidding way. Maybe like a domestic shrine, or a patron saint of hospitality, any spiritual feeling here is more nurturing than threatening. Lives were lived here. For a few moments, ours joined them.

"I'm sorry you're sick, and I'm sorry I'm sick, and I'm sorry for the whole sorry family."

—Lisa, quoting her cousin Mel at a time when both of us were rattling more than rolling.

THE PEAKS

ıe San Francisco Peaks, with atmospherics for decoration.

Peak Effect

Pines and skies and outdoor highs,
peaks to perk a morning's rise,
pine-cone crackle in the smiles
I meet on northern days

sought when I've craved different air—
life as altars without prayer,
arrivals short of getting there—
peaks are what I crave.

I've seen these points from all four sides,
the ups and downs—I realize—
sculpt and shape my own heart's north
in beats between the back and forth.

Climbs and times and walls of wind,
switchbacked turns' relentless spin,
barren shale where top begins,
the summit feeling razed,

a journey I know all too well
strung long by admiration's spell,
heights that call us where we dwell
to merit greater praise—

I've seen these points from every side,
the ups and downs, I realize,
sculpt and shape my own heart's north
in beats between the back and forth.

More than just a showy crest—
memorials to pressure tests—
mountains map the timeless quests
we set ourselves to face,

and, yet, they are less tip than base,
each reach a stretch of sacred space,
rising, rooted deep in place,
source a grounded guide.

I've seen these points from all four sides,
these ups and downs I realize,
sculpt and shape my own heart's north
in beats between the back and forth.

"The Peaks!"
—Julie and/or Lisa, anytime the San Francisco Peaks become visible.

THE PEAKS

They rise above so many of the best places: the Peaks.

Called the San Francisco Peaks by early Spaniards, they are also known as Kachina and Katsina Peaks. Humphreys (the highest point since the volcanic top blew about a quarter of the height off, leaving the gentle caldera, or Inner Basin) is Dook'o'oos'ííd to the Diné, and all area tribes have names for it in their languages as well. Because humans change more than the mountains, calling them by their shorter but undeniable, irrevocable, name works. Besides, the Peaks, like the Grand Canyon, never lead anyone I know to ask "which?" any more than "Elvis" or "the pope" requires further elucidation.

Just as humans changing their name doesn't affect them, the Peaks don't care how high we say they rise. My father has observed wryly that "the Peaks have gotten taller again," or shorter, depending on what the most recent measurement, presumably more accurate than the previous one, pronounces.

In landscape, the Peaks are like the person who walks into the party and makes everyone else seem like supporting cast members. They eclipse anything else in whatever view they occupy, whether it's seeing sunset stain their snow-draped sides across the Verde Valley from the Haunted Hamburger in Jerome, or catching the first sight of them coming from the north: they seem to be physically rising over what looks like flat land as you drive down U.S. 89.

When I was younger, I used to feel sorry for other nearby mountains; surely Kendrick, Sitgreaves, and Bill Williams resented being so completely overshadowed by the Peaks. But then I figured: first, how do I know how a mountain feels; and next, I may as well assume that they love and take pride in a sibling so mighty and dominating. While people seem to know that Humphreys, Frémont, and Agassiz deserve mention as the tallest in descending order, few continue to Aubineau, Rees, and Doyle, all in the eleven-thousand-foot range as well. So the world is full of unknown pecking orders.

Steve Bodinet said, "I've flown in a helicopter to the top of the Peaks, and the view was good. I've hiked to the top of the Peaks, and the view was spectacular."

I've done neither, but I've taken the skyride far enough to see the remaining bits of permafrost that give Arizona a toehold in that geologic zone. I've also flown with former Channel 3 helicopter pilot Jerry Clifton to a meadow on the north side to shoot a piece about fall colors. My father was fortunate enough to be allowed to make that trip with photographer Mike Schmidt and me, and for decades he would mention that adventure on its anniversary. Growing up in northern Arizona, he had generally lived in the Peaks' line of sight, and could remember back when few views of them didn't have snow year-round. The Peaks are where you see the first splotches of gold indicating fall is coming; they cue the aspens to let us know change approaches. That matchless gold is the standard, to me, for all other things called gold.

If all truly important questions can only be answered, "Well, yes and no," the Peaks both change and don't change. On the one hand, they remain stalwart, serene, soaring, no matter where you are in relation to them. Yet conditions prevail upon them to have a thousand faces: the clear stark silhouette from the south at dawn with what my father pointed out a Hopi man had told him was Baby Face. At the far right (east) there's a gentle profile of an infant gazing upward, from the sloping forehead, then the lip and chin as you look down the slope. That sweet image differs significantly from the massive, almost foreboding, snow-covered bulk of the Peaks seen driving in from the west. I love coming across I-40 from Winslow and watching them appear to grow, welcoming me back to Flagstaff. I often recall when a big storm left the top blanketed in white, which a stiff wind turned into what looked like an actual pennant, a banner instead of snow, from the top. And the most common view is, for me, coming up from the south, where they smile regally down on the Verde Valley. My son, Rye, has said that when he was small, he inwardly rolled his eyes at my exhortation to start watching: the Peaks are almost in view, right around the curve . . . there they are! Then, when he began driving up, and especially taking a new passenger, he did the same thing. To me there's a demarcation between being able to see the Peaks and not: I'm instantly more alert and alive, excited and energized, under their benevolent view.

The Peaks, burnished with light during the golden hour.

The first time I read, "I will lift mine eyes up to the hills, from when cometh my strength," it was the Peaks I saw in my mind. When I moved to Flagstaff and could see them from my front door, I made sure to look at them the first thing upon rising, perhaps knowing that view would not be mine forever and I should celebrate them throughout the changing seasons. Finally, I got that elegant line of their silhouette inked upon my left calf, so that I am never without them. They are the only thing I think worthy of marking permanently on my skin, just as they are permanently on my soul, always calling me Home.

"Where do you want to go next?"
—Both of us, again and again.

ABOUT THE AUTHORS

Lisa Schnebly Heidinger grew up knowing her great-grandfather T. C. Schnebly named the town of Sedona after his wife. The delighted great-granddaughter loved Arizona history from an early age (although love of research came only much later). She began telling Arizona stories at the Green Valley News when she was twenty-four. Since then, she's plied her craft in about every way except bard: radio, magazine, television, Sunday op-ed columnist, speaker, and, finally, author.

This is her twelfth book, each about some aspect of her beloved state. (Arizona's official Centennial book, *Arizona: 100 Years Grand*, was voted OneBookAZ, a program sponsored by the Arizona Library and Archives, and as part of its production she made visits to small earnest libraries around the state.)

She thrives on sharing what her father Larry called "the bright bits collected in the crow's nest of the mind," whether it's a former Rockette reminiscing from retirement, or discovering that Sacagawea's son led the Mormon Battalion across southern Arizona.

Since road trips and coffee are up there with storytelling, writing this book has been a Triple Crown of enjoyment. She lives with husband, Tom (Sedona Lee and Rye Schnebly are grown and gone), and dog, Mayer (who followed Happy Jack and Leupp), halfway between Flagstaff and Tucson, with as much time as possible in northern Arizona.

Julie Morrison grew up where her father and his mother did: on a farm in Gilbert, Arizona. The family first grew row crops, most often cotton and alfalfa. Eventually, the alfalfa fed cows in a dairy and feedlot as the family expanded the business. Enough good years later, a cattle ranch in northern Arizona followed. As times changed in the valley, the family developed cropland into houses, and some of those proceeds into schools and professorships at the state's universities.

Seeing her town change to a city sparked Julie's interest in urban planning, which became her first career. Her second was as a cattle rancher in northern Arizona, which she eventually penned into a book, *Barbed: A Memoir.*

When Julie became interested in writing, she contacted Lisa for pointers, and credits Lisa with being the first advocate for *Barbed.* When Julie's writing interests expanded to poetry, Lisa not only kept talking to her, she read the poems.

Julie is a grateful graduate of the Master of Fine Arts in Creative Writing program at Seattle Pacific University. She has lived in six states and in northern, central, and southern Arizona. She now lives with her current dog, Luna.